ANGLICANISM AND EPISCOPACY

A. L. PECK

ANGLICANISM AND EPISCOPACY

A RE-EXAMINATION OF EVIDENCE

With special reference to
Professor Norman Sykes'
Old Priest and New Presbyter

TOGETHER WITH AN ESSAY
ON VALIDITY

LONDON: THE FAITH PRESS LIMITED
NEW YORK: MOREHOUSE-GORHAM CO.

FIRST PUBLISHED IN 1958

PRINTED IN GREAT BRITAIN
in 10pt. Baskerville type
BY THE FAITH PRESS, LTD
LEIGHTON BUZZARD

CONTENTS

FOREWORD

IT will be immediately evident to any reader of Professor Norman Sykes' book *Old Priest and New Presbyter* that he has brought together a most valuable collection of material from a wide range of Anglican and other authorities of the post-Reformation period. Although no such collection could be expected to satisfy every reader on the score of completeness, it cannot be seriously disputed that ample material has been provided from which to trace the lineaments of what has been believed in the Anglican Church about episcopacy during the period under review.

Nevertheless, a first reading of the book led me to doubt whether the conclusions propounded by Professor Sykes were adequately supported by the evidence adduced. His thesis is that there has never been an Anglican 'doctrine' about episcopacy, but only an 'attitude,' which he describes as 'a typical Anglican norm' about episcopacy. This norm is expressed by his assertion that the only ground for episcopacy consistently attested by Anglican writers and formularies is its 'long historical continuance since the apostolic age'; that no particular interpretation of the historic episcopate is justifiable; and that therefore the mere adoption of episcopacy as an historic institution is all that should be required as a condition of full union and intercommunion with the Anglican Church.

A further study of the evidence cited by Professor Sykes convinced me that he had not made good his claim for this Anglican 'norm.' Since Professor Sykes intends his conclusions to be applied to contemporary problems of reunion at home and abroad, it is of immediate practical importance to ascertain precisely what is the content and tendency of the evidence cited by him; and this I have endeavoured to do by means of a careful re-examination of it. I have found that the evidence appears to disclose a much more positive view about episcopacy, and that this view persists through all the post-Reformation centuries in the Anglican Church.

In the second part of the book I have endeavoured to elucidate the meaning of certain terms which occur in Prof. Sykes' book and in the evidence cited by him. Foremost among these is the term 'validity,' which figures prominently in discussions concerning the ministry and problems of reunion; and I have suggested that a more fruitful approach to the question of validity, and indeed to an understanding of what is meant by membership of the Church and of the nature of Holy Orders and of the Sacraments generally, is by means of explicitly personal terminology, in contrast with the legalistic or metaphorical terminology in which such discussions are often conducted. I believe that such an approach may help towards a clearer formulation of the problems and ultimately towards a solution of them which is based not upon compromise, with its negative implications, but upon positive acceptance of what one may, following the persistent post-Reformation Anglican tradition as well as the tradition of previous centuries, claim is the divine will for the Church. It is in this hope that I offer this discussion to my fellow-Christians, both of the Anglican Church and of other communions.

NOTE.—*In view of the very frequent mention of Professor Sykes and of his book in the following pages, I have ventured to use abbreviated forms of reference, which I trust will be readily understood; e.g., 'qd. S., p. 16' is to be read as 'quoted by Professor Sykes,* Old Priest and New Presbyter *(Cambridge, 1956), page 16.'*

PART I

1. INTRODUCTION

I HAVE written this book to provide some assistance for those whose duty it is to make a close study of Professor Sykes' book *Old Priest and New Presbyter,* with a view to forming their own estimate of the contribution which Professor Sykes claims is provided by 'history, that sole upright, impartial referee' towards a solution of present-day problems of reunion. There is, of course, an *a priori* likelihood, when an experienced historian, during the course of a book of 261 pages, prints as verbatim quotations no fewer than 323 separate passages, some of them of considerable length (and this figure does not allow for composite quotations, or for quotations given in the footnotes, or for shorter excerpts embodied in the text), taken from over 120 different authors or authorities, that the conclusions he reaches will be amply and satisfactorily documented. This likelihood cannot, however, be taken for a certainty until the historian's methods have been carefully investigated. The accumulation of quotations does not in itself guarantee that the historian has correctly interpreted the import of those quotations, or that he has taken fully into account the nature of the subject-matter with which the writers are concerned. It is, therefore, in view of the issues involved, of the first importance to assure ourselves upon these two counts, and until we have done this we may rightly hesitate before admitting that the verdict from 'history' presented to us is that of an 'upright and impartial referee.' For if these requisites are lacking, any conclusion drawn cannot be other than partial, in both senses of that word.

In his book Prof. S. undertakes to formulate the typical Anglican 'attitude' to episcopacy, and this attitude he describes (p. 175) as the 'typical Anglican norm.' We shall, therefore, naturally expect to find this norm stated explicitly by, let us say, at least a large minority of the authorities quoted by him; and if we do not find this to be so, it will be legitimate to ask whether the norm formulated has adequate historical basis.

It should further be observed, that whatever norm, if any, emerges from the evidence quoted, it cannot claim acceptance as ultimately valid merely on the ground of its emergence. The Anglican Church has never claimed for itself infallibility, and it has never made such a claim on behalf of any of its theological writers. Any norm which may emerge from a catena of evidence from Anglican writers beginning about the middle of the 16th century must, before it can be accepted as ultimately valid, be measured against evidence from the earlier centuries of the Church's life, and it must also be tested on the score of its own intrinsic merits. These two tests, the 'appeal to antiquity' and the 'appeal to reason,' have indeed come to be regarded and prized as peculiarly typical of Anglican thought. It will therefore be of special interest to observe how they are applied by Professor Sykes.

I should make it clear that I am in no way calling in question the selection of evidence which Prof. S. has presented. Except in five cases,[1] where I have referred to or supplied the context of the quotations which he gives, I have confined my attention to the actual passages which he quotes. There are, of course, other authors whom he might have quoted, but I have made no reference to them, or (apart from the exceptions just mentioned) to any passage of the authors quoted by him other than those actually quoted in his book.

Although Prof. S. sometimes gives the precise date of the passage or incident which he quotes or to which he refers, this is not his invariable practice, and I have taken some trouble to provide the titles and dates [in square brackets] of treatises where he has not provided them. This will, I hope, be useful to the reader, and especially where writers of different periods are quoted in close proximity. I have made a few minor corrections to Prof. S.'s references without comment, where I found them incorrect; though in one or two cases, where the error might cause inconvenience to any one who wished to look up the reference, I have drawn attention to it.

2. The formulation of the Norm

ONE professed purpose of Professor Sykes' book is to ascertain the Anglican view about episcopacy by means of an historical survey. He detects in recent times 'the prevalence of a temper antipathetic to history' (p. 242). This 'antihistorical temper' has penetrated so deeply that there is a danger of abandoning the historical mode of treatment in favour of Manning's axiom that 'the dogma must conquer history' (qd. by S., p. 243). In opposition to this method, Prof. Sykes claims that in his book he follows the true historical method: in the words of Lightfoot (*Philippians* [1868], p. 187, qd.

[1] I have referred to or supplied the context in the following instances:
(1) pp. 7–8: context of the quotation from Swift supplied.
(2) pp. 8–9: context of the quotation from Johnson supplied, and two other incidents referred to.
(3) p. 17: context of quotation from Hooker (*E.P.* VII, v. 10) referred to.
(4) p. 47: context of Sharp's statement supplied.
(5) pp. 71–2: quotations from the Anglican Ordinal supplied.

S., p. 243), 'history is the sole upright, impartial referee.' In pursuance of this rule, Prof. S., by means of copious quotations, traces the views expressed by numerous Anglican writers from the reign of Elizabeth I to the present day.

But, owing to the varied nature of the material, as Prof. S. points out at the end of his chapter on the pre-Tractarian period, 'between such various and contrasting schools of churchmanship it is not easy to discern the *via media* or to attain the highest common factor' (p. 175). And elsewhere, in criticism of others, he speaks of 'the intrinsic limitations attaching to historical evidence, where "probability is the very guide of life" ' (p. 243). There is the danger of seeking 'to dispel historical incertitude by dogmatic presupposition and assertion' (ibid.), and of 'going beyond the historical evidence and imposing dogmatic premisses upon insecure foundations' (p. 245). Nevertheless, in spite of these dangers and limitations attaching to the historical method, Prof. Sykes detects 'the continuance of a typical Anglican norm' (p. 175), 'the prevalence of a norm' (p. 260), on the subject of episcopacy, a norm which he considers that he has so firmly established that he can unreservedly recommend it for adoption by all Anglicans for the future.

The general lines of Prof. S.'s treatment are therefore perfectly clear, but on the details of the application of his method he is less explicit. I think, however, that the following is a fair presentation of the way in which he develops his thesis.

(1) The *definiendum* is 'the typical Anglican norm' on the question of episcopacy.

(2) This norm is to be ascertained by examination of the works of Anglican writers.

It is not entirely clear which are the writers from whose works this norm is to be ascertained. It seems clear, however, that the writers of the first part of the reign of Elizabeth I are to be included. I think that Prof. S. intends also to include writers of the latter part of the reign, for although he writes (p. 58) of 'the more emphatic note which crept not only into the correspondence of English bishops with their continental mentors, but also into the apologetic works which multiplied during the last generation of the reign of Elizabeth I in championship of episcopacy as retained, yet reformed, in the Church of England,' he goes on immediately to say 'The presence of this increased emphasis is not difficult to detect or to defend'; and he has already said (p. 58) that this 'more emphatic note' was 'to be expected' in face of the presbyterian aggression. He therefore appears not to regard it as a deviation from the opinions which had been expressed during the earlier years of Elizabeth's reign; but of this one cannot be absolutely certain.

The qualification of the writers of the following century seems more doubtful. Prof. S. writes (p. 66), 'The Anglican defence of episcopacy became even more emphatic and confident' in the Stuart century; and after citing a good deal of evidence to this effect, Prof. S. then goes on to cite evidence from the same period of 'charitable' views towards the orders and organization of the foreign reformed churches (pp. 69ff.), the purpose of which appears to be to suggest that the emphasis on episcopacy must to some extent be discounted.

The writers of the post-Restoration period are, apparently, still less reliable as authorities for the typical Anglican norm. Here Prof. Sykes speaks of 'innovation': 'It was evident that the outstanding innovation of the Anglican restoration settlement was the unvarying requirement of episcopal ordination for ministry in whatever capacity in the Church' (p. 118).

By the time the Tractarian Movement is reached, he finds writers who are altogether untrustworthy as authorities for the norm. The words of Tract no. 1, says Prof. S., 'testified to the emergence of a new emphasis upon, if not a novel doctrine of, episcopacy in the Church of England' (p. 209).

It appears, then, that the writers of the reign of Elizabeth I, and particularly those of the earlier part of that reign, who wrote before innovations and novel doctrines began to make their appearance, are the most reliable sources for ascertaining what is the typical Anglican norm.

(3) The only definite statement we have from Prof. S. about the method by which the norm is to be arrived at is found on p. 175, towards the end of a chapter which deals almost entirely with the 18th century. Here the method is described in mathematical language as the attainment of 'the highest common factor.' In default of any other explicit statement, we must accept this as a description of Prof. S.'s method, and my general impression is that this is the method which he thinks should be followed. Some support to this diagnosis is afforded by the plan which he follows in Chapter III, to which I have referred above, where after a catena of evidence exhibiting a 'more emphatic note in championship of episcopacy' he gives another catena showing a 'charitable' attitude towards the ordinations of foreign reformed churches.

(4) The norm, as ascertained from the authors mentioned and by the method described, is not a 'theological or doctrinal theory' (p. 244), but an 'attitude' (subtitle on front of jacket). Its content is stated at various points in the book as follows:

(a) Referring to Bancroft, Whitgift and Hooker: 'Episcopacy was defended as being of apostolical, not of dominical, provenance; and the appeal to history and tradition constituted the ground of its justification, not the allegation of any exclusive prescription of scripture' (p. 26).

(b) Referring to Jewel, Whitgift and Hooker: 'Episcopacy had proved itself of divine authority by its continuance from the apostolic age until their own times' (p. 28).

(c) 'Whitgift and Hooker, whilst defending tenaciously the retention of episcopacy on the basis of history and tradition, denied that any one form of government was prescribed in scripture in such wise as to allow of no departure from it' (p. 42).

(d) Summing up at the middle of the 17th century: 'Episcopacy . . . was held to be not of dominical but of apostolic appointment; and as *divino jure* only in that sense; as necessary where it could be had, but its absence where historical necessity compelled did not deprive a church of valid ministry and sacraments. It was necessary to the perfection or integrity of a church, though not to its essence; and on the ground of its historic continuance in the church, its restoration in the foreign non-episcopal churches was much to be desired' (pp. 81–2).

(e) Referring to the same period: 'Thus Anglican apologetic for episcopacy, as necessary where it could be had but its lack not unchurching those churches deprived of it by historical circumstances, adopted the principle of episcopal government and ordination as being of the *plene esse* rather than of the *esse* of the church' (p. 84).

(f) Referring to 'the Tudor and Stuart churchmen': 'Their conviction that, though episcopacy was necessary where it could be had, its absence owing to circumstances of historical necessity did not invalidate the ministry and sacraments of the foreign reformed churches' (p. 94).

(g) As a commentary at the end of the pre-Tractarian period: A quotation from J. Swift, Prose Works, ed. Temple Scott, III, 54, *The Sentiments of a Church of England Man with respect to religion and government* [1708]: 'A Church of England man hath a true veneration for the scheme established among us of ecclesiastic government; and though he will not determine whether episcopacy be of divine right, he is sure it is most agreeable to primitive institution, fittest of all others for preserving order and purity, and under its present regulations best calculated for our civil state' (p. 176).[1]

[1] Since almost the whole of this quotation from Swift is repeated by Prof. S. at p. 261, where with the quotation from Johnson (see (l) below)

(h) 'The Church of England has never set forth any theological or doctrinal theory of episcopacy, but . . . has contented itself with a historical statement of its intention to continue the threefold ministry on the ground of its tradition in the Church since the apostolic age' (p. 244).

(j) 'The traditional Anglican position in regard to episcopacy therefore commends it on the strength of its long historical continuance since the apostolic age, as being of the *bene* or *plene esse* of the Church, and consequently a condition of union of other churches with itself' (p. 245).

(k) 'The Church of England has nowhere formulated any theoretical or theological doctrine of episcopacy; but has contented itself with the assertion of the historical ground of the continuance of the threefold ministry in the Church since the apostolic age' (p. 259).

(l) 'The *via media* affirms the maintenance of episcopacy by the Church of England as part of a continuity with the early and medieval church, its acceptance on the ground of historic continuance since the apostolic age, its requirement for ministering within its own communion, and its restoration to those churches which have lost it, as a condition of reunion, without asserting their non-episcopal ministries and sacraments to be invalid because of its loss' (p. 261 *ult.*). Prof. Sykes then repeats most of the quotation from Swift which he gave on p. 176 (see (g) above), and adds a quotation from Dr. Johnson [1769], who, 'in conversation with Boswell remarked, "Why, Sir, the Presbyterians have no church, no apostolic ordination"; and when asked, "And do you think that absolutely essential, Sir?" replied in modified and mollifying tone, *more Anglicano,* "Why, Sir, as it was an apostolical institution, I think it is dangerous to be without it".'[1]

it forms the conclusion of his last chapter, I have thought it might be of interest to supply the contexts of these quotations. The present passage from Swift continues as follows: 'He should therefore think the abolishment of that order among us would prove a mighty scandal and corruption to our faith, and manifestly dangerous to our monarchy; nay, he would defend it by arms against all the powers on earth, except our own legislature; in which case he would submit, as to a general calamity, a dearth, or a pestilence.'

[1] A somewhat different flavour is imparted to this quotation if we read it in its context (Boswell, *Life of Johnson,* ed. Hill, rev. Powell [I, 103]). Boswell had asked J. whether the fact that his (B.'s) Bohemian servant was a Roman Catholic should prevent his accompanying his master to Scotland. J. had said no. Then B.: 'So, Sir, you are no great enemy to the Roman Catholick religion.' J. 'No more, Sir, than to the Presbyterian religion.' B. 'You are joking.' J. 'No, Sir, I really think so. Nay, Sir, of the two, I prefer the Popish.' B. 'How so, Sir?' J. 'Why, Sir, the Presbyterians . . . (&c., as above; then, after the quotation as given by Prof. S., J. continues): 'And,

It is instructive to trace in this series of formulations of the norm a progressive elimination of positive items and of qualifying statements. Notable among these are (1) that episcopacy was of divine authority, which occurs in (b) and (d) but not later; (2) that episcopacy was of apostolic institution, which occurs in (a) and (d) but not later (unless we count Dr. Johnson; there is, however, in Prof. S.'s own final version no statement that episcopacy was an apostolical institution); (3) the condition that *necessity* is the only ground which will justify failure to retain or to recover episcopacy, which occurs in (d) but not later. No explanation of these omissions is offered.

3. Examination of the Method

I HAVE cited these formulations of the norm as Prof. S. presents them. It will, of course, be our duty to examine to what extent they accurately represent the opinions of the authors whom he quotes; but before doing this we should note that a number of questions are raised by his method of procedure.

(1) First, is it possible to arrive at such a norm, in view of the variety of opinions quoted by Prof. S., a variety to which he expressly draws attention on p. 175? The possibility would not appear to be immediately evident; but it is assumed by him.

(2) Secondly, assuming that the formulation of such a norm is possible, is the method adopted by Prof. S. a satisfactory one? As we have already seen, the method is only once described by him, and then it is described in mathematical terminology as the attainment of 'the highest common factor.' If this means anything in such a context, it presumably means one or other of two things: Either (a) it means the exclusion of everything which is not found in all the views examined, leaving as a residuum that which is common to all of them; or (b), if interpreted on the lines of a *via media,* it may mean an attempt to strike a balance between opposite extremes of view. It is not obvious that such methods, although they may be practicable enough in mathematics, are practicable in a subject such as that with which Prof. S. is dealing. What, for instance, would be the highest common factor if we find on one side an assertion of the parity of ministers, and on the other side an assertion of the imparity of ministers? It is presumably to resolve this problem that Prof. Sykes heads his last chapter 'A Moderate Imparity.' He might, though he does not, adapt for this purpose a well-known dictum,

Sir, the Presbyterians have no publick worship; they have no form of prayer in which they know they are to join . . .' While in Scotland in 1773, J. refused to go to a Presbyterian church to hear a well-known preacher, saying 'I will not give a sanction by my presence to a Presbyterian assembly.' Two years later he attended service in a Roman Catholic church in France.

and say that all ministers are equal, but some are more equal than others.

It is evident that any attempt to arrive at a norm by a strict following of the 'highest common factor' method is impracticable, and the investigator will be forced to rely upon his own discretion in selecting the items which are to be included in the norm. In this case the result will naturally reflect the preconceptions of the person who has constructed it; and the claim that such a norm has been arrived at by 'the historical method' will lose much of its force, for the norm will be based not upon the whole of the evidence quoted, but upon certain selected portions of it and upon the investigator's own interpretation of those portions, and this may be mistaken. When we find that Prof. Sykes in formulating his norm has omitted certain important features which persistently appear in his authorities, we realize how difficult it must be, if one attempts to follow the 'highest common factor' method, to avoid the aberrations condemned by Prof. Sykes himself, when he writes of those who are 'offended by the intrinsic limitations attaching to historical evidence,' and '[seek] to dispel historical incertitude by dogmatic presupposition and assertion' (p. 243).[1]

(3) Thirdly, Prof. S. does not explain why he has chosen the post-Reformation period, and especially the Elizabethan period, and *par excellence* the earlier part of it, as the field in which to look for the 'typical Anglican norm.' This is one of the most remarkable features of his book, and it deserves attention.

'Thus from the outset of its reformation the Church of England continued the episcopal succession and required its ministers to have received episcopal ordination or consecration' (p. 12). In these words, which occur near the beginning of his book, Prof. S. indicates his belief that the Church of England did not begin at the time of its reformation, but was the same Church as before, though reformed. The same view is affirmed, or implied, at the end of the book, where he speaks of 'the maintenance of episcopacy by the Church of England as part of a continuity with the early and medieval Church' (p. 261). This continuity, however, is almost wholly disregarded throughout the intervening part of the book, and it is assumed that the Church of England is a self-subsisting organization, whose history began as it were on a blank sheet somewhere about the middle of the 16th century. It is this narrowing of the field which throws the whole investigation out of proportion. If the Church of England is continuous with the early Church and with the medieval Church in

[1] I hope to show below that there is so great a consensus of opinion among Anglican authorities on the subject of episcopacy that the adoption of the 'highest common factor' method is unnecessary.

this country—if, in fact, it is the same Church—it might have been expected on general grounds that some period other than that immediately succeeding the upheavals of the mid-16th century would have been a more appropriate period for the typical Anglican norm on any subject to find satisfactory expression; and there seems to be no adequate reason for singling out this particularly disturbed period in its history for this purpose. It is, of course, of the greatest interest to ascertain what views were being expressed by Anglican writers at such a period, and it is part of the historian's duty to do this. But that such a period can yield a typical norm is an assumption which Prof. S. has not attempted to justify. Indeed, so far as his conclusions are concerned, the whole of the earlier history of the Church of England might never have occurred. He presents the opinions of writers from the mid-16th century onwards without any background of previous history; they are treated as ultimate data, which cannot be measured by any criterion.[1] This approach can hardly be called 'historical'; indeed, it is almost a negation of the principles of history. It is somewhat as though we were to begin, let us say, the history of English typography at the year 1850, to examine the founts used and the lay-outs adopted between the years 1850 and 1900, and construct a norm of English printing practice from that evidence alone.

(4) Fourthly, such a procedure might be harmless, though mistaken, if nothing further were superimposed upon it. But Prof. Sykes' purpose is not merely an historical survey to enable him to construct a norm; it is to set up this norm as one which is binding upon all Anglicans for all future time; and his conclusions therefore become of practical concern if we are to 'apply the evidence for the historic Anglican attitude towards episcopacy to contemporary problems of reunion abroad and at home' (jacket, inside front). Even if the norm itself were admitted to be sufficiently established as an historical fact, this further point constitutes an additional assumption, for which there is no basis. The historical method may, subject to the limitations enumerated by Prof. S., be able to assure us with some probability that such and such an event occurred, that such and such an opinion was held; but that in itself does not constitute a value judgment upon the event or tell us whether the opinion was a true one. Nor can it assure us that, once it has been established that a doctrine was held at a certain time, or even for a long period, that doctrine was a true and correct doctrine. There was a period when the geocentric doctrine was widely held; but that is no guarantee of its truth. Thus, although 'history' may claim to have established the existence of a 'norm' of Anglican attitude towards

[1] Except in one instance; see below, p. 12.

episcopacy in the 16th century (or even in the 17th and following centuries), it cannot *ipso facto* claim to have told us anything about the quality of that attitude, or to commend that attitude to all future generations as one that must uncritically be accepted. Prof. S. tells us that 'the apologetic position of a church . . . placed in the strait of seeking to repudiate nearly four centuries of its history . . . would be hardly reassuring or sound' (p. 260), and in saying this he is implicitly making such a claim: what has been believed for 400 years must be believed for the next 400, presumably because its truth is thereby guaranteed. It might be more reasonably held that such a church was in a sounder position if it sought to repudiate error than if it persisted in error; but Prof. S. allows for no criterion of truth other than historical duration. Against this there is to be no appeal, either on intrinsic grounds, or on the grounds of Christian experience and practice in earlier centuries. The alleged historic fact that a certain attitude has been held for a particular period of 400 years is to be an infallible and unchallengeable guarantee of its truth. There is a resemblance between this claim of infallibility and one which comes from another quarter, which we may find disturbing. I hope to show later that the fact which Prof. S. alleges is not supported by the evidence which he himself adduces; but at the moment we are concerned only to note the principle upon which he is working, and it is based upon an elementary confusion. To have established by historical methods that an attitude has persisted for 400 years is not the same thing as to have established that that attitude is a true and correct attitude. I apologize for labouring so elementary a distinction; my reason is that Prof. S. has failed to observe it in his book.

It is instructive to notice that there is only one occasion in his book where Prof. S. introduces an appeal to earlier history against the opinions expressed by post-Reformation Anglican writers, which elsewhere are taken as ultimate and basic data, and this is on pp. 239ff., where he wishes to controvert two statements: (a) a statement made by the Committee on the unity of the Church appointed by the 1930 Lambeth Conference that 'the episcopate, as we find it established universally by the end of the second century . . . was, and is, characterized by succession in two forms: the succession in office, and the succession in consecration'; and (b) 'the confident assertion in no. 15 of *Tracts for the Times* [1833–4] that "we know that the succession of bishops, and ordination from them, was the invariable rule of the early Christians. Is it not utterly inconceivable that this rule should have prevailed from the first age, everywhere and without exception, had it not been given them by the Apostles?"' To which Prof. S. replies (p. 241), 'The melancholy answer must be that (the following words he quotes from Dr. W. Telfer, *Episcopal Succession in Egypt, J. Eccl. Hist.* III (1952), 12) "in view of such a history the Tractarian emphasis upon the continuous imposition of episcopal hands will not endure the test of the Vincentian canon".'

Dr. Telfer's conclusion about ordination by presbyters at Alexandria has since been questioned by Canon Kemp (ibid. VI (1955), pp. 125ff.), and the facts still remain in doubt; but elsewhere in his book Prof. S. is not concerned to establish the correctness or falsity of Anglican post-Reformation views when measured against pre-Reformation periods of Church history, and it is difficult to understand what justification there can be for doing so in this isolated instance.

(5) It would appear that the validation of an attitude or an institution by mere 'historic continuance' is a principle which has a strong attraction for Prof. Sykes. He is emphatic that the norm which he claims to have established is not a dogma or a doctrine; there never has been, and there never must be, any Anglican 'theoretical or theological doctrine of episcopacy' (p. 259; cf. the almost identical words on p. 244, 'The Church of England has never set forth any theological or doctrinal theory of episcopacy'). It must, then, be sufficient to assert 'the historical ground of the continuance of the threefold ministry in the Church since the apostolic age' (p. 259). Nothing whatever may be asserted about the threefold ministry except that it has gone on existing; and this, Prof. S. claims, is the Anglican norm. Its basis is merely the historic fact. Episcopacy is to be defended and commended solely as an 'historic' phenomenon, and its acceptance as a condition of reunion must be insisted upon merely 'on the ground of historic continuance since the apostolic age' (p. 261; cf. pp. 244, 245, where almost identical wording occurs). Prof. S. objects to requiring the acceptance of 'a particular interpretation of the historic episcopate and not the adoption of that institution alone' (p. 238). No questions, then, must be asked about what the historic episcopate is, not even why it is historic; all we may say is that it has existed a very long time. It has escaped Prof. S.'s notice that this argument is one that stultifies itself. How, if this is the correct 'attitude' towards episcopacy, did episcopacy ever come into existence? And further, what is the shortest length of time which would enable it to justify itself on the strength of historic continuance? Is it a hundred years, or five hundred, or a thousand? And whatever time we decide on, why does that time justify it, and not half that time? This doctrine of historic aphasia is irrelevant because it cannot explain the historic fact, and I doubt whether it is anything more than a modern *ad hoc*

invention. This doctrine, that there is no doctrine about episcopacy, reduces episcopacy to the status of an irrational and obscurantist superstition; and it cannot be wondered at if intelligent Christians of other denominations consider the insistence upon it as unreasonable, particularly if they themselves can adduce cogent reasons for their own forms of ministry, reasons which are not subject to any such ban of silence. If the Anglican church has only an unreasoning antiquarian prejudice to offer as a basis for reunion, its insistence upon episcopacy will deserve to be treated with contempt. Furthermore, if there is anything which can rightly be described as a distinctive Anglican norm, it is the appeal to reason; and the total exclusion of reason proposed by Prof. S. gives the direct lie to this typical Anglican norm. And it is difficult to understand why this one feature of the Church's life should be exempt from enquiry and explanation when so many others have been submitted to thoroughgoing scrutiny.

We must now enquire whether Prof. S. is justified in attributing the attitude he describes to the Anglican Church, even at the periods with which he is concerned. I do not intend to quote any evidence beyond that which he has himself quoted in his book, with the exceptions already mentioned; and it will be clear from this evidence that most of the authors quoted were prepared to assert something more of episcopacy than that it had continued since the apostolic age. That assertion, indeed, many of them made; but they also made assertions which went beyond the assertion of historical continuance, assertions which contained some significant statement about its nature and authority.

4. The content of the Norm: the Elizabethan period

IN his first chapter Prof. Sykes examines the opinions of the Elizabethan divines, chiefly Whitgift and Hooker, though there are also quotations from Jewel, Poynet, Cooper and Bancroft. This is the period which, as we saw, appears to be the golden period for ascertaining the typical Anglican norm; and as we also saw, the norm as it appears in writers of this period is formulated as follows by Prof. S. (p. 28; formulation (b) above):

> For Jewel, Whitgift and Hooker, therefore . . . episcopacy had proved itself of divine authority by its continuance from the apostolic age until their own times;

but in the later formulations, and particularly in the final formulation of the norm, the reference to the divine authority of episcopacy is omitted. Why is this characteristic of episcopacy, asserted *teste* Prof. S. himself, by Whitgift, Hooker, and others, omitted from his final formulation of the norm? It is difficult to believe that these writers are to be reckoned among those apologists by whom 'the *via media* . . . has not been trodden unswervingly' (p. 260), or that they have 'deviated to one . . . of the extremes' (ibid.); for if these men have erred, who then can have held to the true course? Nevertheless, if Prof. S. has felt obliged to omit their assertion of the apostolic, and even the divine, institution of episcopacy, it must be in order to attain 'the highest common factor' (p. 175). Prof. S. does not explain the principle upon which this process of equalization is to be conducted, nor does he tell us what are the particular deviations which have brought about the omission of these assertions from his final formulation of the norm. We must therefore examine the evidence which he quotes to see whether we can find traces of such deviations. This will also provide an opportunity for checking Prof. S.'s interim formulations of the norm (i.e., (a) to (d) above, pp. 6–7) against the evidence which he quotes.

What, then, are the considerations on the contrary side which Prof. S. may have felt justified him in omitting these important claims made for episcopacy by Whitgift and Hooker?

(1) First, perhaps, is the insistence by writers of the period upon the importance of godly behaviour and sound doctrine on the part of bishops. In order to emphasize this, John Poynet, bishop of Winchester (J. Strype, *Eccl. Mem.,* II, ii, 141, referring to the year 1553; qd. S., pp. 14–15) was willing 'to join for a time' the name *superintendent* with that of *bishop;* and Jewel similarly defended the use of the name superintendent (Jewel, *Works* IV, 906 [*A Defence of the Apology of the Church of England,* 1567]; qd. S., pp. 15–16). Yet Jewel went on to observe that 'the bishops of England have this day not only the same name, but also the same room, and authority, and jurisdiction that other bishops have ever had before.' Prof. S. then remarks, 'In view of this stout insistence on the episcopal succession in the Church of England, it is the more important to observe that Jewel interpreted this succession as one of doctrine, not of sees' (p. 16). This statement is not borne out by the quotations which Prof. S. proceeds to give. Jewel says that succession of sees is not in itself enough; he does not substitute succession of doctrine for succession of sees; he says the latter should be supplemented by the former (or rather, by the maintenance of sound doctrine). For example:

> To be short, we succeed the bishops that have been before our days. We are elected, consecrate, confirmed, and admitted as they were. If they were deceived in anything, we succeed them in place, but not in error. They were our predecessors, but not the rulers and standards of our faith (Jewel, *Works* III, 339 [*A Defence of the Apology,* 1567]; qd. S., p. 16).

In these words Jewel explicitly claims succession of place and of sees; and he claims soundness of doctrine in addition to it, not instead of it. It would be a more accurate comment to say that Jewel, while asserting the succession of sees, pointed out that in addition to this bishops should be men of godly behaviour and sound doctrine. This is not an unreasonable position (indeed, the insistence upon godly behaviour and sound doctrine in bishops has good apostolic precedent); and it is a different position from the rejection of the succession of sees in favour of the 'succession of doctrine' only.

(2) Secondly, Prof. S. emphasizes that 'neither Whitgift nor Hooker abandoned their position that no form of polity is exclusively prescribed in scripture' (p. 17). Again (p. 26), 'Thus, with Bancroft, as with Whitgift and Hooker . . . the appeal to history and tradition constituted the ground of its justification, and not the allegation of any exclusive prescription of scripture.' The suggestion seems to be that these writers were arguing that *episcopacy* in particular is not prescribed in scripture, and therefore, presumably, that it lacks a certain authority which it might otherwise have. We shall, however, be able to estimate this suggestion more accurately if we observe the nature of the controversy in which these writers were engaged. Whitgift was engaged in controverting Cartwright's doctrine of seignories. Hooker, too, was contesting the claim made by the Presbyterians that their form of ministry was exclusively prescribed in scripture. But, as Prof. S. himself points out, Hooker's difference with his opponents was whether 'no form of church polity is . . . to be lawful, or to be of God, unless God be so the author of it that it be also set down in scripture' (*E.P.* III, 2, 1 [1594–7]; qd. S., p. 21). The argument of Whitgift and Hooker, therefore, that no form of church polity is prescribed in scripture, so far from weakening their claims on behalf of episcopacy, throws them into higher relief. Although they did not claim exclusive scriptural prescription for it, they did claim that it was of divine authority; and this as against the claims of their opponents made for the presbyterian polity. We should therefore be wrong if we adopted the suggestion that because Whitgift and Hooker did not claim scriptural prescription for episcopacy they somehow undermined the strength of its position.

(3) Thirdly, there is the statement (S., p. 23) that 'to Hooker, moreover, all good forms of polity, civil as well as ecclesiastical, are established by God.' This judgment, if correct, does not in itself negative Hooker's explicit statement of his belief in the divine origin of episcopacy. Furthermore, it is not evident that Prof. S. is right in suggesting that Hooker arrived at this opinion merely because

of the continuance of episcopacy from the apostolic age to his own times (p. 23). This will be understood if we consider the evidence quoted and the comments made by Prof. S. on p. 23.

> A thousand five hundred years and upward the Church of Christ hath now continued under the sacred regiment of bishops. Neither for so long hath Christianity been ever planted in any kingdom throughout the world but with this kind of government alone; which to have been ordained of God, I am for mine own part even as resolutely persuaded, as that any other kind of government in the world whatsoever is of God Hooker, *E.P.* VII, i, 4 [before 1600]).

'From this historical evidence,' continues Prof. S., and then gives another quotation.

But the latter part of the quotation from Hooker which he has just cited is not historical evidence. The first part is: Hooker recognizes the continuance of episcopacy throughout the ages. The second part, as Prof. S. himself describes it in the line immediately preceding the quotation (p. 22, last line), is a 'doctrine of episcopacy'; and although the consideration of its historic continuance may have confirmed Hooker's belief in its divine origin, that does not appear to have been the consideration upon which his belief was based, as is shown by the third quotation which Prof. S. gives, on p. 23:

> Wherefore, let us not fear to be herein bold and peremptory, that if anything in the Church's government, surely the first institution of bishops was from heaven, was even of God, the Holy Ghost was the author of it (*E.P.* VII, v, 10 [before 1600]).

The immediately preceding context of this passage shows that Hooker was not intending to use a figure of speech when he said 'the Holy Ghost was the author of it.' Hooker quotes instances from the New Testament to show that the Apostles took no important step without a previous direct inspiration from the Holy Ghost; and from this he deduces that they would not have taken a step such as the appointment of bishops without the same inspiration. Prof. S. is therefore mistaken when he comments 'It *would seem* therefore that to [Hooker] episcopacy, *by reason of its historic tradition from the apostolic age to his own times,* had demonstrated its divine authority' (p. 23; italics by me). Hooker's argument is not *ex post facto,* from the later history of the Church; he maintains that the *first institution* of bishops (not their *continuance*) in itself argues direct inspiration from God.

We find a similar line of thought in the passages quoted by Prof. S. from Whitgift, and a similar erroneous comment ('Similarly Whitgift made his appeal to historical tradition in favour of episcopacy,' p. 23). Prof. S. gives three quotations from Whitgift, of which the following are the operative passages:

(1) (Part of an argument against Cartwright) 'This authority, which the bishops and archbishops now exercise, came first from the apostolical Church, then from the example of the primitive Church . . . etc.' (*Works* II, 407 [*The Defence of the Answer to the Admonition* 1574]); and

(2) 'We make no doubt but that the episcopal degree, which we bear, is an institution apostolical and divine; and so always hath been held by a continued course of times from the Apostles to this very age of ours' (Strype, *Whitgift* II, 170 [refers to 1593]).

It is not clear that in these passages Whitgift is arguing back from the continuous 'historical tradition' of episcopacy to its divine institution; and his words are more straightforwardly interpreted as showing that he believed the continuance of episcopacy was due to the fact that it was of divine institution.

We see, then, that a careful examination of the passages cited by Prof. S. shows (a) that they do not contain statements on the contrary side which could reasonably require the omission from the final formulation of the norm of the attribution of divine institution to episcopacy; and (b) that they do not justify the summary which Prof. S. gives at the end of his first chapter (p. 28, formulation (b)), 'For Jewel, Whitgift and Hooker therefore . . . episcopacy had proved itself of divine authority by its continuance from the apostolic age until their own times.' It is particularly important to observe this second point, since the assertion that 'historical continuance since the apostolic age' is the basis of the Anglican view of episcopacy not only persists throughout Prof. S.'s formulations of the 'norm' and appears in his final formulation of it, but appears to the exclusion of the attribution to episcopacy of divine or even apostolic institution.

5. Dissidents from the Norm

In his second Chapter, headed 'A parity of ministers asserted,' Prof. S. refers to only two documents by Anglican writers in which such an assertion is made. There are, however, a few instances of non-episcopal organizations being set up by Anglicans in the time of the persecutions during the reign of Mary Tudor, both in England and abroad, with some comments by Whitgift on the situation in England at that time, and by Hooker on the situation in Calvin's time at Geneva. These, says Prof. S., were 'unusual conditions,' which 'demanded abnormal remedies' (p. 31); we shall not, therefore, expect Prof. S. to have taken them into account in constructing his 'norm.'

Most of the chapter is concerned with the opinions of foreign reformers, e.g. Luther, Calvin, Gualter, Bullinger and Beza (not all of whom by any means asserted a parity of ministers), and there are quotations from the Augsburg Confession and from the Schmalkaldic Articles. The views of the Scottish reformers are also dealt with. Prof. S. cites no Anglican writer who asserted a parity of ministers except Cartwright and the authors [John Field and Thomas Wilson] of *An Admonition to the Parliament,* 1572; the latter, indeed, advocate an 'equality of ministers' in no uncertain language, as might be expected of men for whom the Book of Common Prayer was 'culled & picked out of that popishe dunghil, the Masse booke, full of all abominations' (qd. S., p. 49). There is no doubt, therefore, that Cartwright and Field and Wilson must be reckoned as being on the other side of the *via media* from Whitgift and Hooker, and that they must be allowed their influence upon the norm accordingly. Nevertheless, as a counter-weight to this, Prof. S. finds the Anglican bishops displaying 'a new self-confidence and a more positive assertion of the rights of episcopacy' in writing to 'their foreign mentors' (p. 51); he quotes Bishops Cox and Horne (*The Zurich Letters,* I, 236, no. 94, Bp. Richard Cox (of Ely) to Rodolph Gualter [1571]; ibid. 248, no. 98, Bp. Robert Horne (of Winchester) to Henry Bullinger [1571]).

This chapter, therefore, so far as the construction of a norm is concerned, leaves us very much where we were before.

6. The Norm exceeded?

IN Chapter III, headed 'An imparity of ministers defended,' Prof. S. points out that a 'more emphatic note . . . crept . . . into the correspondence of English bishops with their continental mentors [and] into the apologetic works which multiplied during the last generation of the reign of Elizabeth' (for instance, Thomas Rogers, chaplain to R. Bancroft both as Bishop of London and as Archbishop of Canterbury; writing in 1585 and 1607); and Anglican writers now attempted to show that episcopacy was 'at least not repugnant, and if possible agreeable, to the Word of God; and whilst maintaining its close relationship to the royal supremacy, to have an equal authority with its rival [*sc.* presbyterianism] from the Bible itself' (p. 61). For example, John Bridges, dean of Salisbury, writing in 1587, 'traced the imparity of ministers to apostolic times, and deduced therefrom that episcopacy was of apostolic origin.' Hadrian Saravia (1590 and 1611) 'held bishops to be necessary to the Church, and episcopal government to be the best and of divine authority' (S., pp. 61, 62); 'there could be no doubt of the unequivocal standpoint of Saravia on episcopacy' (S., pp. 62, 63). Matthew Sutcliffe (1591) 'held that "the office of bishops and ministers hath authority and confirmation from God"' (S., p. 63), and 'argued that this form of polity was derived from Christ' (S., p. 63). Thomas Bilson (1593) 'set the coping-stone upon the Elizabethan apologetic for episcopacy' (S., p. 63). 'The episcopal form of polity, thus traditional in the Church,' says Prof. S. (p. 64), 'was not a matter of choice, but of divine appointment.'

Thus, although the association of episcopacy 'with the royal supremacy was still emphasized,' as by Bridges and Bilson (p. 65), 'in the new apologetic episcopacy was finding its own authority and support by appeal to that very Word of God from which Cartwright had quarried his programme of presbyterianism' (p. 66).

7. Two sides of the canvas

'The work thus begun under Elizabeth was continued in the Stuart century, when the Anglican defence of episcopacy became even more emphatic and confident' (p. 66). 'Firmer deductions were drawn from the historical evidence and greater weight placed upon the authority of bishops *divino jure*' (ibid.). Bishop Joseph Hall could say (X, 183 [*Episcopacy by Divine Right asserted,* 1640]; qd. S., p. 66) 'episcopacy is an eminent order of sacred function, appointed by the Holy Ghost in the Evangelical Church.' Archbishop Laud (IV, 310–11 [*The History of the Troubles and Trials,* refers 1644]; qd. S., p. 66) held a similar view. Richard Field 'was peculiar in denying that the episcopate was a separate order . . . notwithstanding, he maintained that "bishops alone have the power of ordination, and no man may regularly do it without them"' (*Of the Church,* V, 704 [1610]; qd. S., p. 67). Bishop Lancelot Andrewes affirmed that 'there is a distinction between Bishop and Priest and that *divino jure*' (*Minor Works,* 29 [*An Answer to the XVIII Chapter of Cardinal Perron's Reply,* written *c.* 1620]; qd. S., p. 67): 'yet at the same time he held that these matters of polity *ad agenda Ecclesiae spectant,* not to the *credenda*' (*Opuscula,* 187 [*Responsio ad Epist. i. Petri Molinaei,* written 1619]; qd. S., pp. 67–8). Even higher ground was taken by Bishop Jeremy Taylor, who held that 'episcopacy . . . should be ranked among the *credenda* of Christianity' (V, 68–9 [*Episcopacy Asserted,* 1642]; qd. S., p. 68). And Prof. S. adds, 'It would be easy to accumulate further evidence of the assertion of episcopacy *divino jure* from the works of Francis Mason, Henry Hammond, Bishop Robert Sanderson,[1] Archbishop

[1] From whose *Episcopacy not prejudicial to Regal Power,* 1647, Prof. S. gives a quotation.

James [*sic; leg.* John] Bramhall, and Herbert Thorndike; but to pile Pelion upon Ossa is needless where the tradition of a positive Anglican apologetic is so strong' (p. 68). And his summing-up is: 'In part . . . this new emphasis upon episcopacy was the result of the dual attack upon the Church of England by Romanist and Presbyterian opponents and of its own afflictions during the Interregnum when the little city of Zoar seemed to have fallen beyond restoration; but it was due also in part to contemporary patristic studies, especially in relation to the First Epistle of Clement, the Epistle of Ignatius, and the works of Cyprian' (p. 69). In this unobtrusive way Prof. S. recognizes that this 'new emphasis' was not merely a reaction against attacks from opponents, but was founded upon the newly available evidence furnished by the patristic writers whom he names. It is, of course, no part of Prof. S.'s scheme to examine the nature of the historical evidence upon which Anglican writers based their opinions[1]; these, as we have seen already, he takes as fundamental data, and does not examine the basis in history upon which they rest; but we have here at least a formal recognition that the 'new emphasis upon episcopacy' was in part due to increased knowledge of the early history of the Church.

Prof. S. now gives what seems to be intended as the other side of the canvas. 'Nevertheless, it is of equal importance to observe that the Anglican asserters of episcopacy generally stopped short of unchurching the foreign reformed churches and of denying the validity of their ministry and sacraments. Episcopacy was the rule and was essential where it could be had; but in cases of necessity it might be dispensed with, and such necessity was judged to be the sad fortune of these churches (p. 69. In passing, we may note Prof. S.'s use of the words 'might be': this, of course, is incorrect, for if the case is really one of necessity there would be no alternative). There is no need at this stage to examine in detail the evidence which Prof. S. quotes. The quotations which he gives make it plain that it was only *inevitable necessity* (the phrase is used by Hooker, VII, xiv, 11 [before 1600]; qd. S., p. 71) which was accepted by Anglican writers as sufficient justification for ordinations in those churches otherwise than by bishops. Here are some examples of phrases from quotations given by Prof. S.: 'the exigence of necessity' (Hooker, ibid.), 'extraordinarily and in case of necessity' (Downham [1608]), '*tamen quod extra ordinem factum est necessitate quadam, paucis quibusdam in locis et uno tantum saeculo, universo orbi legem non praescribit*' (Saravia, *Diversi Tractatus,* 1611). Two cases of exception and necessity are allowed by Richard Field (*Of the Church,* III [1606]): 'wherein all bishops were ex-

[1] He makes only one effective exception to this rule; see p. 12, above.

tinguished by death or fallen into heresy' (quotations in S., pp. 70–3). Hooker acknowledged that 'the Church hath power by universal consent upon urgent cause to take away [the authority of bishops]' (*E.P.* VII, v, 8 [before 1600]; qd. S., p. 70). (I deal with these cases of necessity more fully below, pp. 35ff.)

Views of this sort are considered by Prof. S. in some way to detract from the importance which their authors assign to episcopacy; and, he tells us, 'even more striking admissions' were made by Andrewes with regard to the ministry of the foreign reformed churches (S., pp. 73–4). The two quotations from Andrewes which Prof. S. gives are of great interest and significance. Andrewes says that although the Anglican form is of divine right (*divini juris*), this does not mean that there is no salvation to be had in the foreign reformed churches; nevertheless they do lack something which is of divine right. It is abundantly clear from the quotations which Prof. S. gives that Andrewes' reason for making this 'striking admission' is precisely the same as that of the other Anglican writers: necessity. Necessity had compelled the foreign churches to act thus. 'The fault is not yours but that of the evil of the times' (*Opuscula,* 211 [*Responsio ad Epist. iii Petri Molinaei,* written 1619]; qd. S., p. 74: *id tantum dixi, abesse ab Ecclesiis vestris aliquid quod de divino jure sit: culpa autem vestra non abesse, sed injuria temporum*).

The suggestion that somehow Andrewes, in taking this line, is making a damaging 'admission,' is followed by Prof. S. with three quotations from Hall, introduced with the following words (p. 75): 'Where so staunch a believer in episcopacy as Andrewes had led the way, none need blush to follow. Accordingly Hall's conclusion that episcopacy "for the main substance is now utterly indispensable, and must so continue to the world's end," was qualified by the explanation:

> "indispensable by any voluntary act; what inevitable necessity may do in such a case, we now dispute not; necessity hath dispensed with some immediately divine laws. Where then that may be justly pleaded, we shall not be wanting both in our pity and in our prayers"' (Hall, X, 245 [*Episcopacy by Divine Right asserted,* 1640]).

It will be seen that the 'qualification' consists of the important condition of 'necessity'; and the same point is made by Hall in the other two quotations which Prof. S. gives (X, 282 [*An humble Remonstrance,* 1640]; and X, 152–3 [*Episcopacy by Divine Right asserted,* 1640]), in which we find the phrases 'the necessity of their condition,' and they 'were forced to discard the office [*sc.* of bishop].' The word 'forced' is also used in a similar context by George Downham (*A Sermon defending the honourable function of Bishops* [1608]; qd. S., p. 76); Bramhall (III, 475 [*The Serpent-Salve,* 1643]; qd. S., p. 77) in a most interesting passage, very similar in tone to one of Hall's, says that 'Necessity is a strong plea'; Thorndike (I, i, 92–4 [*Of the Government of Churches,* 1641]; qd. S., p. 80) speaks of the 'necessities' of the state of the reformed churches; he says (V, 426–30 [*A Discourse of the forbearance or penalties which a due reformation requires,* 1670]; qd. S., p. 81), 'It was not of choice, but of necessity, that they embraced that way,' and he speaks of 'the necessity that drove them to it.' Wake, too, in the first quarter of the 18th century, pointed out that Andrewes and others had invoked the cause of 'necessity': 'Our writers still continue to affirm that their [*sc.* the reformed churches'] Orders are not null, though they be not canonical; that their necessity excuses them' (qd. S., p. 82).

In all the authors here quoted by Prof. S., 'necessity' is the only ground which they admit as justifying the loss of episcopacy. We might perhaps, therefore, have expected to find some reference to it in the final formulation of the norm by Prof. S. But, as we have already noted, the reference to 'necessity' as the sole justifying ground is gradually eliminated in his successive formulations of the norm. (See above, pp. 6ff.)

Jeremy Taylor, however, did not even admit the plea of necessity: 'necessity may excuse a personal delinquency'; but he had never heard that 'necessity did build a church' (*Works,* V, 119 [*Episcopacy Asserted,* 1642]; qd. S., p. 78). 'Yet even Taylor,' says Prof. S. (p. 79), 'was not prepared to allow his logic to outrun charity. Although doubting the plea of necessity both on theological and historical grounds, he likewise shrank from unchurching non-episcopal churches.' Thorndike also, says Prof. S. (p. 81), 'placed charity above rubrics' (cf. the quotations above).

Prof. Sykes' phraseology in these comments shows that here, as elsewhere in his book, he has excluded from consideration the nature of the subject-matter with which he is undertaking to deal, otherwise he would hardly have ventured to suggest that the gift of the apostolic ministry is comparable in status with a tiresome and uncharitable rubric.[1] Here, obviously, he is assuming a contrast between, on the one hand, a strict adherence to the letter of a law,

[1] Prof. S. appears, however, to prefer the comparison of the apostolic ministry to a ghost haunting the Church. This is a comparison which occurs twice in his book: at p. 159, 'nevertheless . . . the ghost continued to haunt meetings of the Society [the S.P.C.K.]' (see p. 47, below; and again on pp. 237–8, ' . . . have raised the query whether from the Anglican side episcopacy has not assumed the elusive characteristic of the ghost of Hamlet's father.'

which is rigid and harsh, and, on the other hand, a 'charitable' relaxation of the law, which is reasonable and commendable. Just as previously we found mathematical terminology used to describe the method of ascertaining the norm, so here we find a terminology and an attitude which is inadequate, and even irrelevant, to the subject-matter. If we were in fact concerned with an oppressive law, whose infringement it would be an act of generosity to permit, or if we were concerned with some condition or requirement which had to be complied with before e.g. certain payments could be received, though in some hard cases the requirement might be waived—in such cases Prof. S.'s terminology might perhaps be relevant, and it might be permissible and appropriate to speak of 'admissions' and of 'charity' overcoming the letter of the law. But as soon as we look below this terminology to the realities which it purports to describe, we see that it is wholly inadequate. In the present case we are concerned with gifts of God to human beings; and it is this fact of which Prof. S. allows no awareness to appear in his book. This omission is one of the factors which give an air of superficiality and legalism to his whole treatment. Even if we do not urge the point that episcopacy itself is a gift from God to man, we must at any rate claim that this is true of the dominical Sacraments, i.e. that they are means of grace; and as soon as we replace the mathematical terminology and the language about 'validity' of ordinations and sacraments (as e.g. S. p. 69) by language which speaks of the grace of God, we see how completely reasonable are the 'admissions' which Taylor and others make, and how impossible it would have been for them to say anything other than what they said. What would the alternative have been? To assert that, solely because they were deprived of the apostolic ministry through necessity and through no fault of their own, the foreign reformed churches were cut off from the means of God's grace and from the mutual fellowship which Christians have when associated together in a community. The 17th century Anglicans did not take or assert this view, and we need not be ashamed that they did not take it, nor should we be right in describing their refusal to do so in the terms which Prof. S. uses to describe it. They were simply saying what, from their knowledge of God and from their observation of the reformed churches, they knew to be the truth, viz. that God does not leave His people destitute because through external compulsion they are deprived of the normal ministry and means of grace which He has appointed. It would not indeed be amiss to go further, and to say that even when men deliberately reject those appointed means they are not on that account wholly cut off from the possibility of salvation. To say this is merely to recognize what

God does when exceptional circumstances require it. But none of those 'admissions' has any bearing whatever upon what God's will is for the normal functioning of His Church; and this was fully recognized by the writers whom Prof. S. quotes, although his own method leads him to overlook it. It is his failure to take this into account which makes his whole treatment of the subject unrealistic.

It is therefore no derogation from the high opinion of episcopacy held by Taylor and other Anglican writers of the period that they should 'admit' the grace of God to be operative elsewhere than in a church duly constituted in what they believed to be the divinely appointed way; and hence their 'admissions' to this effect cannot fairly be reckoned as items on the contrary side of the scale, as Prof. S. seems to take them to be.

8. 'Validity'

BEFORE leaving Prof. S.'s Third Chapter it will be advisable to examine the meaning of certain terms which occur in it, and for this purpose we may take as a convenient one the statement on p. 69:

> Nevertheless, it is of equal importance to observe that the Anglican asserters of episcopacy generally stopped short of unchurching the foreign reformed churches and of denying the validity of their ministry and sacraments. (Cf. a very similar statement on p. 81.)

The words 'unchurching' and 'validity' are easy to use in controversial writing, and they are often used without any clear indication being given of their meaning. I have already tried, in the preceding chapter, and elsewhere,[1] to indicate what meaning should be attached to the words 'unchurch' and 'valid' if we wish them to be something more than mere counters in controversy. Unfortunately, no attempt is made by Prof. S. to explain what he conceives to be the meaning of these words; and partly for this reason, and partly because they are used by some of the writers whom he quotes, it is necessary to say something about them.

Prof. S. rightly connects the notion of 'unchurching' with the notion of the validity of sacraments and ministry, for the latter is, clearly, closely bound up with the notion of 'the Church.' Following the lead, however, of the authors of *The Historic Episcopate*,[2]

[1] In *This Church of Christ* (Mowbrays, 1955).

[2] I must here guard against doing an injustice to Prof. Sykes. Since he nowhere acknowledges his debt to *The Historic Episcopate* for the phrase *plene esse*, and since the first of the two courses of lectures upon which his book is based was delivered in 1953–4, *The Historic Episcopate* not being published until 1954, it is possible that the phrase was originated by Prof. S.

Prof. S. uses their negative terminology about episcopacy, and tells us that episcopacy was held to be not 'of the *esse* of the Church,' but only 'of the *plene esse* of the Church'; and indeed the statement that 'Anglican apologetic . . . adopted the principle of episcopal government and ordination as being of the *plene esse* rather than of the *esse* of the Church' forms the culmination of his Third Chapter (p. 84).

Prof. Sykes finds an anticipation of the thesis of the authors of *The Historic Episcopate* in 17th and even 16th century Anglican writers.

(1) Hall (*Works* X, 282 [*An humble Remonstrance,* 1640]; qd. S., p. 75). 'Those particular churches to whom this power and faculty [*sc.* episcopacy] is denied, lose nothing of the true essence of a church, though they miss something of their glory and perfection, whereof they are barred by the necessity of their condition.'

(2) Hall (*Works* VII, 58; *The Peacemaker* [1645[1]]; qd. S., p. 85). 'There is no difference in any essential matter betwixt the Church of England and her Sisters of the Reformation. . . . The only difference is in the form of outward administration; wherein also we are so far agreed that we all profess this form not to be essential to the being of a Church, though much importing the well or better being of it, according to our several apprehensions thereof.'

(3) Bramhall (*Works* III, 518 [*A Vindication of himself and the Episcopal Clergy,* written late 1659 or early 1660, publ. posthumously 1672]; qd. S., p. 76; cf. II, 25 [*A Replication to the Bishop of Chalcedon's Survey,* 1656]; qd. S., pp. 83–4). Bramhall alleged that his opponents' mistake arose 'from not distinguishing between the true nature and essence of a church, which we do readily grant them, and the integrity or perfection of a church, which we cannot grant them without swerving from the judgement of the Catholic Church.' (This distinction, Prof. S. remarks, was taken by Bramhall from a Romanist writer, Thos. Stapleton (1596): Stapleton's

and communicated by him in discussion to the authors of *The Historic Episcopate;* it may, perhaps, have been derived from Stapleton's phrase (see p. 27). He does not, however, include the phrase in his final formulation of the norm; and indeed he differs on at least one fundamental point from the authors of *The Historic Episcopate,* whose Editor in his Introduction (p. 8) urges that Anglicans must be able to 'show the Nonconformists a *theological* interpretation of episcopacy' [his italics]. Prof. S., as we have seen, stoutly denies that there is any such thing as an Anglican 'theological or doctrinal theory of episcopacy' (S., p. 244), and it may be for this reason that he does not include a term with so technical a sound as 'of the *plene esse*' in his final formulation of the norm.

[1] It may be useful to place on record that the entry in *S.T.C.,* no. 12698 of a 1624 edition of *The Peacemaker* is incorrect. The work published in 1624 was a sermon entitled *The True Peacemaker,* as correctly stated in *S.T.C.,* no. 12715.

distinction was between the *intrinseca et essentialis Ecclesiae definitio* and the *plena definitio seu potius descriptio*. That the distinction he drew was not quite of the sort we might have been led to expect is shown by the fact that in the *plena definitio* Stapleton includes such items as *incipiens a Jerusalem* and *crescens per omnes gentes;* qd. S., p. 84, n. 1.)

(4) Earlier still, in 1574, Whitgift (*Works* I, 185; qd. S., p. 83), had written: 'Notwithstanding government, or some kind of government, may be a part of the Church, touching the outward form and perfection of it, yet it is not such a part of the essence and being, but that it may be the Church of Christ without this or that kind of government.'

First, it must be remembered that these statements were made with churches in mind which had been deprived of the Apostolic ministry through 'ineluctable historical necessity' (S., pp. 126, 241); they are therefore to be read and understood in that context, and they cannot therefore fairly be reckoned as relevant material towards the construction of an 'Anglican norm' with regard to episcopacy. Nevertheless, Prof. S., in giving an interim formulation of the norm at the end of his Third Chapter, says that 'Anglican apologetic . . . adopted the principle of episcopal government and ordination as being of the *plene esse* rather than of the *esse* of the Church' (p. 84). To describe this as a 'principle' is to go far beyond what the evidence warrants, for the reason admirably stated by Saravia: *Quod extra ordinem factum est necessitate quadam, paucis quibusdam in locis et uno tantum saeculo, universo orbi legem non praescribit* (see above, p. 21). It would be more aptly described by Prof. S.'s own word 'attitude' than by the term 'principle': it was an attitude adopted in face of an abnormal situation. It was left to modern writers to convert this *ad hoc* attitude into a universal Anglican 'principle of episcopal government . . . being of the *plene esse* rather than of the *esse* of the Church.' This view, however, Prof. S. finds so congenial that in spite of his assertion that the Church of England has never had any doctrinal theory about episcopacy (see pp. 238ff.), he does not hesitate to affirm that Anglican apologetic adopted it as a *principle*.

We must, then, be careful to remember that when the Anglican writers quoted by Prof. S. state their opinions about the continental reformed churches they are not purporting to lay down a doctrine about normal church government or about episcopacy in particular. They are attempting to express in words the abnormal situation in which certain Christians found themselves when they were prevented by 'ineluctable historical necessity' from exercising the divinely appointed ministry. Their attitude is admirably summed up by some phrases in a remarkable passage from Bramhall (*Works* III, 475–6 [*The Serpent-Salve,* 1643], qd. S., p. 77): 'Where we are not sure that there is a right ordination, what assurance have we that there is a Church? . . . I dare not limit the extraordinary operation of God's Spirit, where ordinary means are wanting, without the default of the persons. He gave His people manna for food whilst they were in the wilderness. Necessity is a strong plea. . . . It is charity to think well of our neighbours, and good divinity to look well to ourselves. . . . I know that there is great difference between a valid and a regular ordination; and what some choice divines do write of case of necessity; and for my part I am apt to believe that God looks upon His people in mercy with all their prejudices; and that there is a great latitude left to particular churches in the constitution of their ecclesiastical regiment, according to the exigence of time and place and persons, so as order and His own institution be observed.'

This is a valuable passage, for in it Bramhall uses the terms 'Church' and 'valid' (distinguishing 'valid' from 'regular'); and elsewhere he defends the English divines against a charge that they 'unchurched' the Protestant churches. We saw also that he drew a distinction between 'the true nature and essence of a church' and 'the integrity or perfection of a church'; the continental churches had the former, but were deprived of the latter.

This leads to the second point: What is the meaning of this language? Or, more precisely, what is the only meaning which can give an intelligible sense to it? Surely this. The Church is the society where the redemptive power of Christ is operative through the means which He has appointed. Occasions may arise when men are forcibly deprived of these means. In such circumstances God does not allow Himself to be thwarted, but continues to tend His people in their tribulation. It is therefore legitimate to describe their ordinations and sacraments as 'valid,' because God effectually uses them to convey His grace to His people; and such a body of Christian believers can be called a 'church,' because God uses that society as the sphere is which His redemptive power operates. The Good Shepherd ensures that His flock is fed; and that is why Bramhall can say that they have 'the true nature and essence of a church.' God gives His people manna whilst they are in the wilderness; their food is still supplied. But they will not expect manna when they have escaped from the wilderness; to do that would be presumptuous as well as unreasonable. Manna is an emergency expedient, to ensure that God's people remain alive: no argument about God's normal provision can be founded upon His action in such a situation.

The term 'valid' is a dangerous one because we are accustomed to use it in contexts far different from religious ones, and we tend to assume that it applies there in the same sense as it does in business contexts. If we wish to take a train journey there is only one sort of ticket which is valid, namely, that issued by the railway authority, purchase of which is the only method of obtaining the particular service of conveyance over a particular stretch of line. The term 'valid' could also be applied to a banknote. In all such cases the basic factor is the backing which the ticket or the note possesses, viz. the competence and willingness of the authority in whose name it is issued to supply what it signifies; and the difference between a valid ticket or note and a forgery is that the latter is designed to enable its possessor to obtain something from the issuing authority against its will (and usually to its financial disadvantage). A ticket or banknote might also be 'invalid' if the issuing authority lacked the resources required to make good the services to which it ostensibly claimed to entitle the holder. It will at once be seen that such situations cannot arise in the case of sacraments. It cannot be supposed that God is either incompetent or unwilling to supply that which the sacramental sign claims to convey. God has no interest, financial or other, in preventing His gifts from being freely available to mankind. Impediments to the reception of them can lie only in the recipient, and not in the supplier, i.e. in the recipient's inability to take full advantage of what is supplied. In this limited aspect we might cite the illustration of a gramophone record, which has the ability, when played, to convey the full meaning of the composer's music to any one who hears it; and it makes no difference who puts the record on the gramophone. It would be ridiculous to pretend that the record can be heard only when a certain person or class of persons has put the record on. The case is similar with any work of art. All these are means by which the author or composer is able to convey to the listener or viewer something of his own personality, and that indeed is one of the important features about sacraments: they are independent of any virtue on the part of the celebrant or performer of them, just as the virtue of the record is independent of the virtue of the person who places it on the gramophone, and the virtue of the work of art is independent of the virtue of its exhibitor. We must, then, refuse to use commercial language when speaking of sacraments; and 'valid' is a word which, as commonly used, can hardly fail to imply such commercial associations. Neither the nature of God the supplier nor the nature of that which he supplies permit the use of terminology which is appropriate only to commercial transactions. The only intelligent and relevant meaning we can attach to 'valid' when used of sacraments and ordinations is that God is able and willing to use them to convey His redemptive power to men; and it cannot be supposed that, however irregular these sacraments and ordinations are, God refuses outright to use them if men perform them in good faith, whether constrained by force, or misled by ignorance and sin. 'Validity' depends not upon man, but upon God, who is the only validator of any sacrament. We shall therefore make no progress towards reunion so long as we continue to attempt to distinguish between 'valid' and 'invalid' sacraments, classing some as 'invalid' because of some alleged defects on the human side in the immediate circumstances of their performance. Nor will it help to quote others as alleging, or ourselves to admit or maintain, that the ordinations and sacraments of non-episcopal communities are 'valid'; for God's ability and willingness cannot be in doubt: all, in virtue of His ability and willingness, are 'valid.' The question to which we must address ourselves is not Are these sacraments valid?, but, What is the divinely appointed method with regard to orders and sacraments?; and that is why Prof. S.'s final formulation of his norm (p. 261) is inadequate and irrelevant: it speaks of requiring the restoration of the episcopate 'to those churches which have lost it, as a condition of reunion, without asserting their non-episcopal ministries and sacraments to be invalid because of its loss,' but it does not include the assertion that the episcopal ministry is the divinely appointed method. As we saw earlier, that assertion, made by the 16th century Anglican divines, is eliminated by Prof. S. from his final formulation of the 'Anglican norm.' But ultimately there is no other cogent reason for 'requiring' churches, whose ministries and sacraments one admits to be 'valid' without episcopacy, to accept it. If, like Prof. S., we maintain that the Church of England has no 'theological or doctrinal theory of episcopacy' (p. 244), we can only fall back, as he does, on 'the ground of historic continuance' (p. 261 and *passim*); and although the non-episcopal bodies cannot claim a ministry which has had historic continuance 'since the apostolic age,' some of them can claim a continuance of substantial duration, and the longer they continue the stronger their ground of historic continuance presumably becomes. On a mathematical basis (and what other basis have we for reckoning 'continuance'?), the non-episcopal ministries are in a much stronger position than they were 100 years ago, and the comparative strength of their position *vis-à-vis* episcopacy is continually increasing, though at a diminishing rate.[1]

[1] See Appendix, p. 102. It should be noted that Prof. Sykes' phrase 'continuance since the apostolic age' is not an oversight for 'continuity with the apostolic age'; and in one place (p. 245) this is emphasized by his addi-

It will be seen from these considerations that it is irrelevant to label certain ordinations and sacraments as 'invalid,' meaning thereby that they are automatically 'inefficacious,' i.e. incapable of mediating the grace and power of God. It is for this reason that the arguments adopted by Roman Catholics to discredit the Church of England are also irrelevant. They are irrelevant because they leave out of account the nature of the subject under discussion, and ultimately because they leave out of account the nature of God Himself.[1]

Nevertheless, a term is certainly required to describe orders and sacraments which (according to whatever the view is which one adopts) are 'regular' (Bramhall's word, see above, p. 28); and it is true that for this purpose the term 'valid' can claim a certain appropriateness—to this extent, that it unmistakably suggests that something of fundamental importance is involved. On this score it has the advantage over 'regular' and 'canonical,' which suggest a much less fundamental standard of reference: 'uncanonical' sounds much less terrifying than 'invalid'; and it may be that controversialists prefer the term 'invalid' as being a more potent bogey. What is needed is a term which, while possessing the suggestion of fundamental importance that 'valid' has, avoids the mechanical implications which have come to be associated with that term, and at the same time avoids the suggestion that a merely legalistic and organizational matter is involved, which is the disadvantage of 'canonical.' Indeed, we may incline to think that all terms of this sort are inadequate and misleading, inasmuch as they disguise the true nature of the matter which they purport to describe. I would suggest that the only adequate description to apply to 'regular' orders and sacraments is 'divinely appointed.' This description has, in addition, several advantages:

(1) It draws attention to the real point of difference between the various Christian bodies, for no doubt all of them, whatever their belief on this subject, would claim that their own form of church order most closely represents the divine will. If not, there is no ultimate reason for maintaining it against other forms.

(2) It draws attention to the positive side of each type of belief, and does not provide an easy and depreciatory opposite (like 'invalid') to be applied to other sorts of ministries with the implied suggestion that they cannot be 'efficacious,' for, although they may not be appointed by God, they may be used by Him.

tion of the adjective 'long'—'its long historical continuance since the apostolic age.' 'Long *continuity with* the apostolic age' would of course be meaningless. Prof. Sykes' phrase has been carefully chosen so as to exclude the notion of *continuity with* the apostolic age, which might be taken to imply a doctrine of apostolic succession. See also p. 72, below.

[1] This subject is dealt with more fully below; see Part II.

(3) Even more than 'valid,' it emphasizes the fact that something of fundamental importance is involved.

(4) It suggests how the various types of belief are to be tested.

How does one ascertain what is the divinely appointed order for the Church? Some hold that it is papacy; some episcopacy; some presbyterianism, and so forth. The traditional Anglican criterion is a twofold one: the appeal to antiquity, and the appeal to reason; but to neither alone. Neither a bare fact nor a bare logical construction has any cogent authority. And if a man is honestly and sincerely convinced on these two grounds that presbyterianism is the divinely appointed form of ministry, he cannot be expected to assent to another or to adopt it unless it can be shown to him that the proposed alternative is more satisfactory on these two grounds. Similarly a Papist, if he wishes to convince an Anglican, must be able to show the superiority of papacy on these two grounds.

It is the second of these two traditional Anglican standards which is completely ruled out by Prof. S., ostensibly because he fears that any 'doctrine' which might be formulated would do more than assert the bare historical facts. But such an objection might be brought against any doctrine, for the purpose of a doctrine is to formulate the significance of the facts. The doctrine of the Trinity, for example, does more than state the bare facts as recorded in history; it is a formulation of the significance of those facts. It is an entirely unwarranted assumption that any doctrine about episcopacy must be 'anti-historical.' It is not axiomatic that in this case 'the dogma must conquer history'; the dogma may state the significance of the history, and then it is entirely legitimate.

I think, however, that Prof. S. is prompted, consciously or unconsciously, to rule out this second standard by a further consideration. He thinks that, if he can confine our attention to the bare historical facts alone, he can bring forward instances of historical facts which overthrow any doctrine which we may adopt, and particularly the claim which is made on behalf of episcopacy. But in this connection it must be remembered that the formulation of a doctrine is not in all respects parallel to the formulation of a scientific theory. One fact to the contrary is sufficient to disprove a scientific theory. But even if it could be shown that on one occasion, or on half a dozen occasions, there had in the early days of the Church been non-episcopal ordinations, the doctrine that episcopacy was the divinely appointed order would not necessarily be disproved. It would be no disproof of the doctrine of the Trinity to show that a considerable number of Christians for a considerable time had not accepted it. Nor would it necessarily disprove a doctrine if it could be shown that it was not explicitly and clearly formulated during the first two or three centuries of the Church's history. It cannot in any case be supposed that the Church in Jerusalem in the days immediately after Pentecost had formulated in doctrinal terms the truths by which its life was lived. Here again, then, it is essential to remind ourselves of the nature of the subject with which we are dealing, and not to apply methods which are appropriate to a different field of investigation. The application of inappropriate methods is a mistake which is made in this connection by Prof. S. (see pp. 240–1). The method which he uses is a method which is appropriate to the formulation of a scientific theory on the basis of observed natural phenomena. It would be admirably suited to a subject such as chemistry or physics. There is no reason why we should agree to its use in the present case.

Furthermore, if we are willing to allow the appeal to reason in our consideration of episcopacy, we shall not need to share Prof. Sykes' fear of being led 'as easily and logically to the papal claims as to those of an episcopal apostolic succession' (p. 245). Prof. S. quotes, apparently with approval, a passage from a book by E. C. Rich (*Spiritual Authority in the Church of England*, p. 194): 'Looked at from a strictly objective standpoint both the doctrine of apostolic succession and the doctrinal claims of the apostolic see are in the same category; they can only be justified and insisted upon in accordance with presuppositions concerning the nature of the Church and her ministry' (qd. S., p. 245). It is not necessarily correct to assume that these, or any, doctrines are founded upon presuppositions; indeed, it would seem that Christian doctrines, at any rate, cannot be of this nature. There is much evidence to show that the main Christian doctrines were produced as attempts to formulate the significance of facts already given and known; and there is no evidence to show that episcopacy emerged as the result of any presupposition or as the result of a logical process of ratiocination. It is entirely legitimate to hold that any doctrine of episcopacy was produced, as other doctrines were produced, in order to formulate the significance of a fact already experienced. In such a case the application of reason to the experienced fact or phenomenon may well provide us with a doctrine which will throw light on the nature of the Church itself. It may be that the fact of episcopacy, when understood, will even give us the key to the understanding of the nature of the Church, and that the nature of the Church cannot be fully understood without it. Prof. S. offers us no indication of what his doctrine of the Church is, or how he arrived at it. Since, however, he tells us that episcopacy is not 'of the *esse* of the Church,' he has presumably arrived at his own doctrine of the Church without taking episcopacy into account. Before we can allow that he is justified in this course, we shall need to know what method he has in fact adopted, and we have so far no guarantee that his doctrine of the Church is not founded upon some presupposition.

We must not expect, then, that any form of ministry will be justifiable solely on logical grounds (its basis is not merely a 'doctrine'); nor can it be justified solely on the basis of fact ('historical continuance'). This statement will, of course, hold good of papacy and episcopacy alike; but it does not follow automatically that the historical facts about both, and therefore that the doctrines about both, are identical: it would indeed be a surprising coincidence if they were; and it is the exclusion of any examination of the character of the doctrine about episcopacy—on the ground that *any* doctrine must falsify the facts—which leads Prof. S. to endorse the opinion that the claims of papacy and episcopacy are 'in the same category'—viz. that they must be founded upon presuppositions—and ultimately to the conclusion that there must be 'no doctrine about episcopacy.'

9. 'Necessity' and 'Necessary'

We have already traced the implications of the term 'valid,' and a similar result will be obtained if we trace the implications of the term 'necessity' (and its adjective 'necessary'), which figures prominently in Prof. S.'s Third Chapter and in some of the quotations in it. It is perhaps somewhat unfortunate that this term is there used in two quite different senses, although in practice they can be easily distinguished. They both appear in Prof. S.'s summing-up on p. 81:

> [Episcopacy] was held to be . . . necessary where it could be had, but its absence where historical necessity compelled did not deprive a church of valid ministry and sacraments. (Cf. a statement in almost identical terms on p. 94.)

A similar statement, but with the word 'essential' in place of 'necessary,' is found on p. 69:

> Episcopacy was the rule and was essential where it could be had; but in cases of necessity it might be dispensed with, and such necessity was judged to be the sad fortune of these [*sc.* foreign reformed] churches.

We distinguish here two different modes of 'necessity':

(1) The necessity on account of which certain Christian bodies were obliged to abandon episcopacy.

(2) The necessity of episcopacy itself, which necessity, according to some of the authorities quoted by Prof. S., may be overruled by the former mode of necessity.

Although it is the latter of these two 'necessities' with which we are now concerned, it may be useful first to examine more closely than was done above (pp. 21ff.) what actual examples of the former 'necessity' are mentioned by the writers quoted by Prof. S.: what situations would, in their opinion, justify the plea of 'necessity,' warranting the abandonment of episcopacy?

(a) The first example—he calls it 'a very hypothetical case'—quoted by Prof. S. is from Hooker, VII, 5, 8 [before 1600]; S., pp. 69–70): 'The whole body of the Church hath power to alter, with general consent and upon necessary occasions, even the positive laws of the apostles. . . . The Church hath power by universal consent upon urgent cause to take it [*sc.* the authority of bishops] away, if thereunto she be constrained through the proud, tyrannical, and unreformable dealings of her bishops.' Again (ibid. VII, 14, 11; S., p. 70), '. . . There may be sometimes very just and sufficient reason to allow ordination made without a bishop. The whole Church visible being the true original subject of all power, it hath not ordinarily allowed any other than bishops to ordain; howbeit, as the ordinary course is ordinarily in all things to be observed, so it may be in some cases not unnecessary that we decline from the ordinary ways.' These cases, as stated by Prof. S., quoting the words of Hooker, are:

   (i) 'where God raised up special agents whose mission He authenticated "by manifest signs and tokens from heaven,"' and

   (ii) '"the exigence of necessity . . . where the Church . . . neither hath nor can have possibly a bishop to ordain. . . . These cases of inevitable necessity excepted, none may ordain but only bishops."'

(b) Downham's 'cases of necessity' were: 'a church either altogether destitute of a bishop, or pestered with such as the popish prelates are, heretical and idolatrous' (*Sermon,* 1608; S., p. 71).

(c) Saravia, though not mentioning 'necessity' in the passage quoted by Prof. S. (p. 107, n. 1), remarks on the contempt into which the 'Roman Antichrist' and his satellites had brought the very title of Bishop [1611].

(d) Field (III, 154–71 [1606]; S., p. 73) 'alleged two cases of exception and necessity, namely, "wherein all bishops were extinguished by death or fallen into heresy."'

(e) Andrewes (*Opuscula,* 211 [1619]; S., p. 74) spoke of 'the evil of the times. . . . France did not have kings so favourable to the reformation of the Church as did our England.'

(f) Hall (X, 245, 282, 152–3 [1640]; S., p. 75) spoke of 'inevitable necessity . . . churches to whom this power and faculty is denied . . . whereof they are barred by the necessity of their condition.' They 'were forced to discard the office, as well as the men; but yet the office because of the men; as popish, not as bishops.'

(g) Downham, again (*Sermon,* 1608; S., p. 76) says the foreign Protestants 'were forced with the loss of the episcopal government to redeem the most precious jewel of the Gospel.'

(h) Bramhall (III, 475 [1643]; S., p. 77) wrote: 'Necessity is a strong plea. Many Protestant churches lived under kings and bishops of another communion; others had particular reasons why they could not continue or introduce bishops.'

These examples quoted by Prof. S. indicate clearly the grounds which these Anglican writers believed were sufficient to sustain a plea of 'necessity' for discarding episcopacy or for dispensing with episcopal ordination; they may be summed up as follows:

(1) Irreformable corruption on the part of the bishops (Hooker); heresy, idolatry, etc. on the part of the bishops (Downham, Field, Hall; cf. Saravia).

(2) The physical absence of any bishop who might ordain (Hooker, Downham, Field).

(3) Political pressure (Andrewes, Bramhall; perhaps also Hall); and

(4) Manifest signs and tokens from heaven (Hooker; this appears to apply only to cases of exceptional individuals).

The nature of these four types of necessity may be stated as follows:

(1) Compulsion of internal circumstances (i.e. conscience—the inability to approve erroneous doctrine or morality on the part of the required agent), but ultimately due to external circumstances.

(2) Compulsion of accidental external circumstances—absence of the required agent.

(3) Compulsion of deliberate external circumstances—force applied by others.

(4) This contains no element of compulsion, and therefore strictly speaking is not a case of 'necessity' at all. Nevertheless, consideration of this type of case helps us to understand the real nature of the other three, as well as this. All are, essentially, cases in which the 'necessity' (in the other sense of 'necessity') of episcopacy is rendered inoperative. It would therefore be less confusing if the term 'necessity' in the sense we are now discussing were replaced by a less ambiguous and indeed more appropriate description, e.g. 'a situation overriding, or overruling, the necessity of episcopacy.'

The second mode of 'necessity' differs from the first in that it does not prevent the performance of some act, but enforces or enjoins its performance, either for its own sake, or as a condition for the achievement of some further objective. But again it is not immediately obvious how this mode of 'necessity' applies to episcopacy. In what sense can it be asserted that episcopacy is 'necessary'? And if it is necessary, how can there be exceptions? How can it be said that 'episcopacy is necessary *where it can be had*'?[1] Is not this a contradiction in terms, and if not, why not?

In common usage, 'necessary' denotes that which is inevitable or indispensable; or something which cannot be 'done without' if some further result is to be achieved. It is applied to that which is inevitably fixed and determined by natural laws, and to what inevitably results from the constitution of things. If A is done, then it is necessary that B results; or if B is to occur, then it is necessary that A first occurs. In such cases, the possibility of any exception is completely ruled out. Since the 'necessity' of episcopacy appears to admit of exceptions, episcopacy cannot be 'necessary' in this sense. And, indeed, it could hardly be maintained that episcopacy has the status of a natural law.

The term 'necessary' can, however, be applied not only to what is enforced by some natural law, but also, by transference, to that which is enforced by some human law or human agency, either for the sake of the thing itself, or as a condition of attaining some further result. This resembles the previous case, but the degree of inevitability is not so complete, for no human agency can have the force of a natural law. The effectiveness of this 'necessity' depends upon the power of the compelling agent to enforce his will, or upon his power to prevent the attainment of the ultimate result without compliance with the conditions he has laid down. Is episcopacy 'necessary' in this sense? It is, of course, possible to conceive of a civil or ecclesiastical authority enforcing episcopacy as a mere institution by means of a civil or ecclesiastical enactment (indeed, it has been done); but to enforce it in this way as a precondition of receiving the benefits which are believed to derive from it (e.g. divine grace) is not within the competence of such an authority, although, again, ecclesiastical authority has made that claim. But apart from this consideration, it would appear that something of greater binding force is implied in the statement that 'episcopacy is necessary where it can be had.' The obligation implied appears to be a more powerful one than any which could be imposed by any civil or ecclesiastical authority. And our clue to the problem lies in the consideration of something which has just been men-

[1] Cf. above, pp. 21, 34.

tioned, viz. the benefits which are believed to derive from episcopacy.

If, then, we consider *for what purpose* episcopacy is held to be 'necessary,' we shall be able to recognize the nature of the 'necessity,' and the source from which that necessity comes. Prof. S. summarizes the view of many of the Anglican divines when he writes (p. 81), '. . . but its absence where historical necessity compelled did not deprive a Church of valid ministry and sacraments.' ('Necessity' in this sentence is, of course, used in the first sense already examined.) The purpose, then, of episcopacy, or one of its purposes, was to ensure a 'valid ministry and sacraments.' Yet, where episcopacy *could not be had,* the ministry and sacraments were still valid. This can only mean, as stated by Thorndike (V, 430 [*A Discourse* etc.], 1670; qd. S., p. 81), that 'God accepteth of their ordinations, though not made according to rule, in consideration of the necessity that drove them to it.' That is to say, God fulfils His purpose of conveying sacramental grace to men in those exceptional circumstances, although the sacraments are administered by non-episcopally ordained ministers. And this implies that the normal method, i.e. the method by which God wills to do it, is through the episcopally ordained ministry.

The meaning of the statement 'episcopacy is necessary' is now clear. It can only mean that 'episcopacy is divinely willed and appointed.' And at the same time we can see why, although episcopacy is 'necessary,' it may in some circumstances be 'dispensed with'—by God: it is because when God sees that men are unable, by no fault of their own, to follow the divinely appointed way, He can and does provide by exceptional means what they would otherwise have received from Him by the divinely appointed means.[1]

There is, of course, nothing strange about this conclusion. It is exactly what we should have expected. If the purpose of episcopacy is to provide for the conveyance of God's grace to men, we should expect the 'necessity' of episcopacy to lie in God's appointment of it. It is therefore clear that the only intelligible meaning which can be attached to the term 'necessary' in Prof. Sykes' summing-up is 'divinely willed and appointed'—which is in fact precisely what the term was understood to imply by many of the authors whom Prof. S. quotes. To say that 'episcopacy is necessary' without elucidating and emphasizing the real meaning of 'necessary' disguises the full implication of the statement and can lead only to confused

[1] It may be urged that this is open to objection as an overstatement if pressed in detail; but it is important not to allow such objection to override its fundamental truth. I shall argue below (in Part II) that it is wrong to particularize in too great detail about what is effected through any sacrament.

thinking. It is, of course, true that Prof. S. wishes to eliminate the notion that episcopacy is of divine appointment; but if it is 'necessary' in any intelligible sense, it can be necessary only in the sense that it is divinely willed and appointed. It is the only meaning of 'necessary' which fits the case.

We can now restate in more informative language Prof. Sykes' assertion (p. 81) that according to the Anglican divines episcopacy was 'necessary where it could be had, but its absence where historical necessity compelled did not deprive a church of valid ministry and sacraments.' We can substitute for 'necessary,' 'necessity,' and 'valid' the meanings which we have elucidated. The statement, then, put into plain language, means: The episcopal ministry was the divinely appointed ministry; but when certain Christians found themselves, through no fault of their own, in circumstances where that ministry was not available, or where they could avail themselves of it only by violating their consciences (i.e. by condoning corrupt morals or what they believed was corrupt doctrine on the part of those who held that ministry), God made up to them so far as possible what He would have supplied if that ministry had been available to them.

Such a reformulation of the statement avoids the use of counters whose meaning may be unknown or ambiguous.

The result of our investigation of the meaning of the three terms may be summarized as follows:

(1) The term 'valid,' if it is to be applied to orders and other sacraments, should be used only to denote that they derive their validity from God and are used by Him to convey His grace and power.

(2) The term 'valid' should not be used in the sense of 'regular' or 'canonical,' but should be replaced by 'divinely appointed.'

(The use of the term 'valid' as applied to the immediate technical requirements of form, matter and intention, should be discontinued; and the use of 'valid' in the sense of 'papally authorized' should be rejected.)

(3) The term 'necessary' as applied to episcopacy means, and should be replaced by, 'divinely appointed as requisite for man's salvation.'

(4) The term 'necessity,' as applied to historical circumstances, describes a situation in which the requirement to observe the divinely appointed ordinance of episcopacy is held to be overruled by certain specified causes.

It will be seen that these are the meanings of the terms as used by the Elizabethan divines quoted by Prof. S., and that these meanings are sometimes quite explicitly stated, sometimes clearly implied. But even if it could be shown that they are not clearly implied in all cases, it is still true that they are the only meanings which make sense of the attitude adopted by those divines, and further that they are the only meanings applicable to the subject itself.

We should also note that the terms are applicable in other contexts also, in these same senses. For example, in the phrase 'matters necessary to salvation' in the passage quoted from Bancroft (*Sermon*, 1588; qd. S., p. 25), 'necessary' will bear the same meaning as when it is applied to episcopacy. It affirms that these matters are appointed by God as requisite for men's salvation; it does not automatically exclude the possibility of attaining salvation without them by special action on the part of God.

Furthermore, we must be careful, when we find these terms used by later writers, to examine them in the light of our recent investigation. This applies especially to the term 'valid.' In this connection, Prof. Sykes' treatment of the Tractarian view in Chapter VIII is a case in point. It is part of Prof. Sykes' contention that the 'Tractarian emphasis on the *exclusive* validity of the orders and sacraments of episcopal ministries' was a 'novelty' (p. 212). But unless we are to interpret this 'emphasis' as being intended to deny any efficacy whatever to non-episcopal ministries, we are now able to see that to assert that episcopal ministries and sacraments are exclusively the valid ones is to assert that they are exclusively the divinely ordained ones; and there is nothing particularly novel about this assertion. If, however, it were maintained by Prof. S. that the Tractarians intended to go further than this, i.e. to call in question the use by God of non-episcopal ministries, then we must consider that the situation in the 1830's was far different from the situation in the earlier periods to which Prof. S. refers; and it could not unreasonably be urged that when the 'necessities' (such as political pressure, corruption on the part of bishops, etc.) no longer operated, it would be presumptuous for men to continue expecting that God's graces would still be available extraordinarily, otherwise than through the divinely appointed means, and there could be nothing unreasonable (or novel) in pointing this out, and in urging them to accept episcopacy. Prof. S. draws attention to what he calls the 'novelty' of the Tractarian emphasis and to the 'gulf [which divided] them from their seventeenth-century predecessors' (p. 213), without at the same time drawing attention to the fact that the circumstances which gave rise to the 17th century views had ceased to operate in the 19th century. Indeed, so far from being 'novel,' the Tractarian view was stated in very similar terms by George Smalridge in 1708 (qd. S., p. 126), when he wrote (referring to the question of the Protestant churches of Prussia—the very subject on which Prof. S. contrasts the views of the Tractarians with those of the earlier writers: 'We should be importunate with them to receive episcopacy; and if, after being called upon and shown that the reception of it is practicable, they will still obstinately refuse to embrace it, we shall not be obliged to entertain the same charitable opinion of them, which we and those who have gone before us have hitherto done.' Upon this Prof. S. comments (ibid.), 'This frank statement was equally important as testimony of the general allowance made by high-churchmen for the foreign reformed churches traditionally in the past, and as evidence of a desire to make an end to temporizing and pleas of ineluctable historical necessity by pressing upon them the duty of restoring episcopacy, now that it could be had from an unimpeachably reformed source in the Church of England.' If there is any difference between the view of Smalridge and that of the Tractarians on this point, it is that Smalridge is somewhat the more outspoken, and it is difficult to see how it is possible to go on representing as a 'novelty' a view which had been forcibly expressed over 120 years earlier. Prof. Sykes' error here is due partly to his failure to understand what is meant by 'validity,' and partly to his persistently ignoring the qualifying condition of 'necessity' which was the only ground on which the 17th century Anglican writers admitted the 'validity' of non-episcopal orders and sacraments, i.e. they held that circumstances had arisen in which it could be believed that God waived His divinely-appointed requirement of episcopacy, so that such orders and sacraments were used by Him.

10. Charitable Sentiments in Practice

In his Fourth Chapter Prof. S. deals with the translation of the 'charitable sentiments' of the English divines into actuality.

'From the outset it was clear that the Church of England would not surrender its own episcopal government in the interests of the union of Protestants' (p. 85). In conference at the Synod of Dort in 1618, Bishop Carleton (in his own words, qd. S., p. 86), 'showed that by Christ a parity was never instituted in the Church,' and that bishops were appointed by the Apostles to succeed them.

Prof. S. then deals with the question whether presbyterially ordained ministers from the foreign churches were admitted without episcopal ordination to benefices with cure of souls in the Church of England during the three quarters of a century between the accession of Elizabeth I and the Civil War. He examines the well-known cases of Dr. Peter de Laune (1618 and following years) and of Caesar Calandrinus (1620 to 1639). Of the former, Prof. S. says (p. 91), 'It appears highly probable therefore that de Laune did not receive episcopal ordination during his clerical career, but the matter is not capable of positive proof'; of the latter he says 'That Calandrinus continued after institution without reordination seems clear' (p. 93). Although these 'two swallows indeed do not make a summer' (S., p. 93), Prof. S. claims that the Anglican representatives on a joint committee of Anglicans and Freechurchmen in 1925 'did somewhat less than justice both to the historical evidence and to its interpretation' when they spoke of 'the confused times of the 16th and 17th centuries,' and said that such exceptions 'form a very insecure basis of precedent.' Prof. S. holds that these exceptions were merely the 'translation of precept *and principle* [italics by me] into practice' (p. 94); and regretfully adds, 'The paucity of such cases was the natural consequence of the circumstance that . . . the Church of England recruited its ministry predominantly from "the English by nation as well as in church discipline"' (S., ibid.).

The next question is whether the Church of Scotland was regarded as a *foreign* reformed church: could that church plead 'necessity' as an excuse for presbyterian ordination? Hooker [1594–7] was inclined to think it could; Laud (1639–40) thought it could not. Grindal in 1582 had licensed John Morrison, presbyterially ordained in Scotland, to officiate throughout the province of Canterbury, though apparently not to have cure of souls. Wake, nearly 150 years later, 'refused to disavow, whilst unable to approve, Grindal's action' (S., p. 98). In 1610 three bishops were consecrated in London for Scotland without previous episcopal ordination as priests.

Professor S. comments, on p. 106, 'Throughout the Anglican references to foreign reformed churches there recurs the refrain of historical necessity, which had caused them unwillingly and involuntarily to abandon episcopacy. This, however, was challenged directly by Jeremy Taylor'—as we have already seen.

Towards the end of the chapter there is a paragraph pointing out why many of the leading reformers 'jettisoned the episcopal order': it was because 'the medieval papacy had brought episcopacy into such discredit' (pp. 106–7); and further, 'in the political conditions of the 16th century, successful defiance of the papacy and reform of the Church were impracticable without the active championship of the godly prince' (p. 107).

The outcome of Prof. Sykes' review, then, is that very little was done, or at least very little is definitely known to have been done, in the way of translating the charitable sentiments of the English divines into actuality. No doubt this was because they were not asked to do very much, and it is useless to speculate about how they would have acted if they had been asked to do more. It is clear from the evidence that the sentiments resulted directly from the 'necessity' which evoked them, and the only question would be how far the permanent effects of that necessity (viz. a man's status as presbyterially ordained and not episcopally ordained) would still qualify to evoke the same response once he had reached this country. It does not follow that the same procedure would have been adopted if there were a large number of such cases as might be adopted for a few, before the need had arisen to work out an agreed practical method of dealing with them.[1] In any case, we cannot fairly reckon the sentiments evoked by the abnormal conditions of 'necessity' as contributing towards the construction of an Anglican 'norm.'

II. Innovation, Latitudinarianism, and Diversity

IF we now take a review of Prof. S.'s first four chapters, it may appear to us that he has not accurately gauged the significance of the Anglican apologetic for episcopacy during the period so far examined. In view of the prevailing circumstances, including those in continental countries, it would not, perhaps, have been surprising if Anglican writers had shown some considerable hesitancy on the subject of episcopacy, and therefore the firmness of their attitude acquires the greater significance. From the very beginning of the period we find the apostolic and even the divine origin of episcopacy clearly asserted, and in practice we find no exceptions to episcopal ordination apart from the few somewhat doubtful 'swallows' cited by Prof. S. in Chapter IV.

But in Chapter V we come to an 'innovation.' No more swallows were to be permitted to fly: 'the outstanding innovation of the Anglican restoration settlement was the unvarying requirement of episcopal ordination for ministry in whatever capacity in the Church' (p.118). In 1610 'the Church of Scotland had been accorded quasi-recognition as a foreign reformed church, labouring "under a real necessity"'; in 1661 'it was regarded as being "in a state of schism," and that of its own deliberate contrivance' (p. 120). With regard to the Protestant churches of Prussia, George Smalridge,

[1] On this subject, Dr. Woodhouse writes as follows (*The Doctrine of the Church in Anglican Theology 1547–1603*, London, 1954, p. 193), 'Nevertheless, from the evidence found in the Bible, primitive practice, and by the authority of the Fathers, all these Anglican divines in this period regarded bishops as necessary—save in very extraordinary cases—to safeguard the faith, to ordain and confirm and to stop schism. While they accepted the plea of necessity in the case of other Churches, one cannot say that they would regard it as valid if it had lasted four hundred years.'

afterwards Bishop of Bristol, in 1708, as we have already seen, 'expressed the opinion that "we should be importunate with them to receive episcopacy; and if, after being called upon and shown that the reception of it is practicable, they will still obstinately refuse to embrace it, we shall not be obliged to entertain the same charitable opinion of them, which we and those who have gone before us have hitherto done"' (qd. S., p. 126). Prof. S.'s comment upon this I have already cited (p. 41, above).

Dr. William Nicholls, canon of Chichester, writing to Prof. Pictet of Geneva in 1708, explained that at ordination no one was obliged to swear on oath that he accepted episcopacy as ordained by divine right (S., p. 127). Archbishop Wake (1720) assured Prof. Turrettini of Geneva that the 36th Article of the Church of England did not affirm 'the necessity of the three orders which we retain in our church' (ibid.). Prof. S. records, however (p. 122), that 'in the case of Mr. James Horner he [Wake] confessed to Père Le Courayer, his Gallican correspondent,

> I have ordained Mr. Horner both deacon and priest; and thereby received him into the ministry of the Church of England. This is a work that gives the most offence of any to the other Reformed Churches; but I must agree with you that I know no government older than Calvin's time, but what was episcopal, in the Church of Christ.'[1]

Wake expressed similar views to Arthur Charlett in 1707; see the quotation on p. 45, below. In commenting on the passage relating to Horner, Prof. S. writes (p. 122), 'The principal defence offered to assuage such scruples was to explain the requirement of episcopal ordination as both the result of the Act of Uniformity and as a domestic rule of the Church of England which involved no judgement on the validity of the presbyterian orders of the foreign reformed churches.'

During the series of conferences in 1668 'the grand stop in our treaty,' according to Richard Baxter, 'was about reordination' (p. 130), and Bishop Wilkins would not accept a formal statement that presbyterian ordinations were valid. In 1689, the royal commissioners, who reflected 'contemporary opinion amongst men of latitude,' and were appointed to present to Convocation and to Parliament a project for the Comprehension of Presbyterians and Episcopalians in the Church of England, made proposals for conditional reordination of presbyterian ministers. These proposals, however, 'were never debated in Convocation, owing to the un-

[1] *Biographia Britannica,* VI, part 2, p. 4094; letter dated January 14th 1722–3 (reference and date given by N. Sykes, *William Wake,* II, p. 19). The ordinations were in November and December, 1722.

favourable reception which it was anticipated they would encounter' (S., p. 133).

On the subject of 'the healing custom' of occasional conformity, Prof. S. recalls that in 1702 Edmund Calamy, leading a deputation of Dissenters to Bishop Burnet, mentioned that occasional communion 'had been used by some of the most eminent of our ministers ever since 1662, with a design to show their charity towards that church, notwithstanding they apprehended themselves bound in conscience ordinarily to separate from it'; 'not quitting their own ministry, or declining the exercise of it as they could have opportunity' (qd. from E. Calamy, S., pp. 138–9). This practice was approved by Whig prelates such as Archbishop Tenison and Bishops Patrick and Burnet, and by 'the high-church tory Archbishop Sharp of York' (*Letters of eminent men to Ralph Thoresby* [I, 273 f., March 1697]). 'But although the latitudinarian temper of the 18th century was favourable to the continuance of such practices, it did nothing positively to further the design of "comprehension"' (S., p. 140), presumably because the Dissenters had conscientious objections, though what these were is not shown by Prof. S. Dr. Chandler 'went so far as to offer that, whilst none of his presbyterian brethren would renounce their ordination, yet "if their lordships meant only to impose their hands on us, and by that rite recommend us to public service in their society or constitution, that perhaps might be submitted to"' (qd. S., p. 140 [from a letter by J. Barker to Doddridge, dated Feb. 2nd, 1748. 'Their lordships' were the Bishops of Norwich (Gooch) and Salisbury (Sherlock)], *The Correspondence and Diary of Philip Doddridge*, ed. Humphreys, V, 43). Presumably, therefore, their lordships meant something more than that. Thomas Secker [then Bishop of Oxford], though sympathizing with Doddridge's desire for comprehension, told him that he saw 'not the least prospect of it' (qd. S., pp. 140–1 [from a letter dated February 21st, 1745], *The Correspondence*, etc., IV, 382).[1]

In 1707, Archbishop Wake, writing to Arthur Charlett, considered the case 'vastly different between communicating with the Protestants abroad and our separatists here at home, yet I believe no one who could have the opportunity of an episcopal church in foreign countries would make any doubt whether he should choose to partake of some of the Gospel ministrations with that or with those of the presbyterian way.' He also remarked that 'they cannot except against our ministry nor the validity of the ordinances which may be supposed to depend upon it. Our clergy are certainly duly

[1] Prof. S. gives the reference as IV, 272, but this is to a different letter, also from Secker, dated 1743.

ordained, whatever theirs are who want episcopal ordination.' And further, 'I cannot think them so conformable to, at least, the apostolical pattern and establishment, as if they were settled on the same episcopal constitution as our church is' (Ballard mss., III, fo. 83; qd. S., p. 142). Gilbert Burnet [speaking as Bishop of Salisbury in the House of Lords on the Occasional Conformity Bill in December 1703] said that he had been 'an occasional conformist in Geneva and Holland,' though he had 'thought their churches irregularly formed' (Cobbett, *Parliamentary History,* VI, col. 163; qd. S., p. 142). 'There was indeed,' writes Prof. S. (p. 143), 'a well-established tradition of the welcoming to communion in the Church of England of foreign Protestants, both Lutheran and Reformed, when visiting England.' Among them were the Prince of Orange and his retinue, and ministers and others of the Dutch churches. John Cosin, during the Commonwealth times, joined with the Protestants in Paris and baptized their children 'at the request of their own ministers' (*Works* IV, 397–8 [*Answer to Mr. Fuller's Charge,* 1658, referring to *c.* 1645], qd. S., p. 144). Some of them also frequented the Anglican public prayers and received communion, and some of their students were presented to be ordained priests and deacons by the Anglican bishops. Wake, while in residence as chaplain to the Embassy in Paris, attended every other Sunday at Charenton, but did not receive the Holy Eucharist there. On the other hand, he gave communion to 'some of their ministers publicly in their own chapel' (qd. S., p. 145). 'Such,' says Prof. S., 'were the customs established before the revolution of 1688' (p. 145).

In 1705 the Church of Geneva, thinking itself to have been aspersed by an Oxford academic exercise entitled *Strenae Oxonienses,* made a protest and averred that it had always had a singular esteem for the Church of England. In 1706 the University of Oxford made a formal reply, in which it was pointed out that they did not condemn those Reformed Churches '*quae, ineluctabili necessitatis lege adactae, a primaeva Episcopalis regiminis forma haud sponte sua recesserunt. . . . Hanc nos disciplinam auctoritate plusquam humana fundatam, ac divina providentia per omnia quae ab Apostolorum usque temporibus fluxerunt saecula ad nos transmissam, non sine singulari Dei beneficentia retinemus* ; and they went on to point out that the Reformed Cause would more readily prosper, and opposition to the Pope be more effective, '*si . . . conjunctis sub antiqua apostolici regiminis forma copiis militaremus*' (qd. S., pp. 147–8). This, says Prof. S., 'expressed exactly the standpoint of contemporary high-churchmen.' 'Equally typical' was the negotiation for uniting the Lutheran and Reformed Churches in Prussia on the basis of an episcopate to be derived from the

Anglican bishops (1683 and following years). Bishop Wake, writing to J. Le Clerc of Amsterdam, J. F. Ostervald of Neuchâtel, and Peter Zeller of Zurich (*c.* 1716), urged the reintroduction of episcopacy, and the Moravian Brethren he recognized as a true episcopal church. Wake also approved reciprocity of communion between Anglicans and the reformed church of Zurich in anticipation of their reintroducing episcopacy. He was, however, disappointed by the Swiss, who showed 'no readiness to adopt [episcopacy] in their own churches' (S., p. 153); he received formal compliments about the Church of England, but no suggestions for practical action.

Bishop Cosin (*Works* IV, 407 [Letter to Mr. Cordel at Blois, dated Paris, February 4th, 1650] qd. S., p. 151) had told Mr. Cordel that he might go 'otherwhiles to communicate reverently with them of the French church'; Ussher (C. R. Elrington, *Life*, p. 260, qd. S., p. 151 [*c.* 1649]) had expressed his willingness to receive communion from Dutch ministers in Holland and from French at Charenton; Sharp [1704] said he would do the same in Protestant churches abroad[1] (qd. S., pp. 151–2). Dean Granville of Durham (later a non-juror) advised communicating with the French reformed, on the ground that they 'were at their first reformation, and are still, in such circumstances that they could not then retain [episcopacy], nor can have it now, if they would' (R. Granville, *Life of Dennis Granville*, 202–3; qd. S., p. 152; [? 1678]). On the other hand, during the Interregnum, Bishops Bramhall and Sydserf and Dr. George Morley and Richard Steward had declined to do this. George Hickes (later a non-juror) did so *c.* 1673 at Charenton; he afterwards changed his mind.

It would appear at first sight that Prof. S. attaches great importance to the action of the S.P.C.K. in South India during the 18th century, when owing to a curious chain of circumstances the Society was employing Lutheran clergy in default of English missionaries. The work was begun in 1705 by King Frederick of Denmark and Prof. Francke of Halle in Saxony; two Lutheran divines, ordained by the Danish bishop of Zetland, were sent out. As a result of the marriage of Queen Anne to a Danish prince, the support of the S.P.G. for this missionary work was invited, but that Society's charter did not permit such work, and it was undertaken by the

[1] Prof. S. does not, however, record that Sharp refused a request made on behalf of M. Claude Grosteste de la Mothe, a French minister in London, to allow the publication of this statement (which he had made in the House of Lords during a debate on the bill of Occasional Conformity); he refused probably because (as his biographer says) misleading deductions might have been made from the statement by those who did not consider 'the difference there is between the case of the Protestant Churches abroad, and our dissenting congregations here in England' (T. Sharp, son of the Archbishop, *The Life of John Sharp*, ed. Thos. Newcombe, 1825, I, 379).

S.P.C.K. in connection with the German-Lutheran mission at Tranquebar. The propriety of this action was queried in 1713 by a former Secretary of the Society. Archbishop Wake, however, as President, approved of it. In 1735 an ordination of a native catechist by Lutherans in India raised afresh the question of non-episcopal ordinations, and the General Meeting of the Society gave its approval to what had been done. Clearly, from the quotations given by Prof. S., Henry Newman, the Secretary, was a warm supporter of the policy, and must have been largely responsible for its persistence. Some of the missionaries were ordained by Lutherans, some by Danish bishops. Nevertheless, despite the 'impeccably latitudinarian sentiments' repeatedly expressed by Newman, 'the ghost' continued to haunt the meetings of the Society, and the question came up again in 1779. In 1791 the annual report stated that there ought to be suffragan bishops in the country who might ordain deacons and priests, 'and secure a regular succession of truly apostolical pastors, even if all communications with their parent church should be annihilated' (H. J. Cnattingius, *Bishops and Societies,* p. 47; qd. S., p. 160). (This last phrase, incidentally, is of particular interest in view of recent developments in South India.) A Secretary of less impeccably latitudinarian sentiments held office from 1785 to 1823 (George Gaskin); in 1814 an Anglican bishop was appointed for Calcutta, and the policy of the Society was changing. The last German-Lutheran was appointed in 1818, two other missionaries having been ordained that same year by the Bishop of Zetland, and 'there was,' says Prof. S., 'a recurrent and growing uneasiness as the century progressed on the part of some members of the Society as to the propriety of its continuance of the custom . . . and . . . the patronage and employment by the S.P.C.K. of the German-Lutheran ministers, though a recognition *de facto* of the validity (as distinct from the regularity) of their orders, did not imply an acceptance of them *de jure*' (p. 164). In 1825 the decisive step was taken by Reginald Heber, the second bishop, who ordained three Lutherans employed by the C.M.S.

Prof. S. gives some quotations to illustrate Bishop Heber's views on episcopacy; these are taken from his introduction to his edition of the works of Jeremy Taylor ([1822]; S., pp. 165–7). The substance of them is this: Jeremy Taylor was wrong in asserting 'the absolute necessity that some form of church government should be found laid down in scripture,' but 'the apostles . . . thus commissioned by Christ and thus guided by the Paraclete, delegated to three different orders of men distinct and different portions of the authority which they had themselves received. . . . And it is plain that not only is the fact that episcopacy was instituted by the followers of Christ and the possessors of the Holy Spirit, sufficient to prove it neither an irrational nor unchristian form or polity, but that a very great and evident necessity must be shown, before any human hand can be authorized to pull down or alter a fabric erected under such auspices. . . . Though I am far from confounding the relative value of institutions immediately authorized by Christ, immediately tending to the salvation of souls, or of visible and universal advantage to them, with those which respect ecclesiastical order, it can hardly I think be denied that those churches are wisest who retain episcopacy; those sectaries least excusable who dissent from it; and that the authority of apostolical tradition cannot reasonably be rejected in this case, without endangering many other observances of Christianity which are almost universally accounted *essentials*' (italics by me).

The comment by Prof. S. which follows immediately (p. 166) seems somewhat unexpected, but it must be conceded that it is masterly in its boldness: he writes, 'It is difficult to interpret these statements otherwise than as indicating that Heber held episcopacy to be of the *bene* or *melius esse* of the Church rather than of the *esse;* representing thereby the traditional pre-Tractarian high-church position.' A further quotation from Heber, given by Prof. S., makes it quite clear that he held the same view as the earlier Anglican divines about necessity: he pointed out in answer to criticism, 'You suppose that I *generally* admit ordination by Presbyters to be valid. I do not admit this. All I said is that, when a Christian nation has, *by unfortunate circumstances,* lost its apostolical succession of bishops, those good men are not to be censured who perpetuate it by the best means in their power' (*Narrative of a Journey through the Upper Provinces,* 1828, qd. S., p. 167; italics by me). The nation which Heber had particularly in mind was Germany. Here again Prof. S. has converted into an absolute and *unconditional* principle a view which as expressed by Anglican writers is qualified by certain very clearly stated *conditions.*

Prof. S., in his comment on Heber's statement, thus makes a further addition to the series of *esses:* his contribution is 'of the *melius esse.*' No explanation is offered of the relation to each other of *bene esse, melius esse,* and *plene esse,* and no indication is given of what is to be understood by 'of the *esse* of the Church.' Heber's own statement, that the rejection of episcopacy can hardly fail to endanger many other Christian observances which are almost universally accounted *essentials,* is scarcely distinguishable from an assertion—if we must use such terminology—that episcopacy is 'of the *esse* of the Church.'

The 'time of ignorance' (if, as Prof. S. seems to intend, we may apply his chapter-heading to one particular instance with which he deals most fully) in South India lasted only just over 100 years, and therefore falls appreciably short in duration of the historical continuance of 400 (or is it 1500, or 1900?) years which Prof. S. has adopted as his standard measure; indeed, he himself tells us that 'there can be no doubt that this [i.e. the provision of bishops, who might secure a regular succession of truly apostolic pastors] represented the long-term policy and ideal of the Society' (p. 160). It is difficult therefore to know how much weight he intends to allow this occurrence in settling the balance of his norm; all we can say is that his account of it occupies over 13 pages out of 261 in his book.

Between 1714 and 1832, Prof. S. finds 'the widest diversity of opinion amongst English churchmen concerning . . . the necessity of episcopacy' (p. 167). For example:

Benjamin Hoadly [1717], Bishop of Bangor, was decidedly to the left of the *via media:* he 'denied that Christ had delegated authority to any officers in the Church' (p. 167); he 'had subverted all claims to authority on behalf of the episcopate' (p. 168). William Paley supported the distinction of orders in the Church on the ground that it corresponded to the different orders in secular society: it was able 'to supply each class of people with a clergy of their own level and description, with whom they may live and associate upon terms of equality' (*Sermon* III [1782], *Works,* ed. Chalmers, V, 35 f., qd. S., p. 169). William Law, replying to Bishop Hoadly, 'set forth a classic defence of the high-church position' (p. 169): 'an uninterrupted succession is as necessary, as that the clergy have a divine commission' (W. Law, *Three Letters* [1717]); qd. S., p. 170). John Wesley moved 'to a belief and practice of presbyterian ordination' (1746; S., p. 171). 'An equal latitude prevailed amongst many of the Anglicans who were caught up by Whitfield's Calvinistic movement' (p. 172): e.g. Thomas Haweis (1800): 'whether episcopacy, a presbytery, or the congregational order be established as the dominant profession, it affects not the Body of Christ (qd. S., p. 173). In 1796 some Evangelical Anglicans joined with Calvinistic dissenters to found the London Missionary Society, which prescribed no particular form of Church government. In 1799 the C.M.S. was founded, maintaining the Anglican tradition of episcopacy. The Clapton sect stood firm against all aberrations with respect to episcopacy. Bishop George Horne of Norwich 'laid down the principle that the divine ordinances cannot be administered "to effect but by God's own appointment; at first by His immediate appointment, and afterwards by succession and derivation from thence to the end of the world"' (*Works* II, 570;

qd. S., p. 173). William Jones of Nayland held that 'the fact is therefore undeniable, that the Church has been governed by Bishops, Priests and Deacons, from the Apostles downwards' (*Works* V, 31 [*An Essay on the Church*, 1787]; qd. S., p. 174). Archdeacon Charles Daubeny was 'more rigid and extreme': 'what form of government the Apostles agreed to establish in the Church, if not expressly communicated to them by Christ in person, must be considered established under the direction of the Holy Spirit' (*Guide to the Church* [1798]; qd. S., p. 174)—in which he followed very closely in the steps of Hooker (cf. above, p. 17); Bishop Van Mildert defined the Church 'as existing under that apostolical form of government which from the date of its first institution, it has invariably exhibited in the far greater part of the Christian world. It is the Church episcopally constituted. . . . Without entering into controversy with those who deny the divine origin of episcopacy, it can hardly be disputed that . . . the catholic or universal Church . . . was known and distinguished by its episcopal constitution' (*Theol. Works* IV, 223, Bampton Lectures [delivered 1813]; qd. S., p. 175).

12. The Nineteenth Century: Tract I and afterwards

WITH Prof. Sykes' Seventh Chapter ('Giant Pope') we are not now directly concerned, since his norm is not constructed with a view to furthering reunion with the Roman Catholic Church. But his eighth and last chapter ('*Via media:* a moderate imparity') would seem relevant, for it is there, according to the summary on the dust-cover, that he 'applies the evidence for the historic Anglican attitude towards episcopacy to contemporary problems of reunion abroad and at home.' In fact, the Eighth Chapter is something of a miscellany.

It begins with the eunciation of one of Prof. Sykes' favourite themes, the 'novelty' of the Tractarian doctrine about episcopacy; passes on to deal with various reactions to the Jerusalem bishopric proposal (1841), the Sumner-Phillpotts incident (1851), the controversy about the 'united communion' of the Revisers of the translation of the Bible (1870) and the Kikuyu controversy (1913–14); a few decisions in cases where the admission of unconfirmed persons to communion was sought (1897 and 1900); the resolutions of various Lambeth Conferences and Committees; negotiations with the Church of Scotland (1932–4; resumed 1947); the Malines Conversations (1921–6); a brief reference to the bull *Apostolicae curae* of 1896[1]; negotiations for intercommunion between the Church of England and various continental episcopal Churches, including Orthodox Churches (1936–51); the attitude of the Lambeth Conference of 1930 to the South India unification proposals and the failure of the 1948 Conference to approve full intercommunion, indicating the dominance of the 'novel' Tractarian doctrine over the 'traditional Anglican' doctrine; an appeal to early Church history to counteract this doctrine as expressed in Tract No. 15 and in a pronouncement by the Lambeth 1930 Committee on the Unity of the Church; and an attack on the 'anti-historical temper,' culminating in a twice-repeated reassertion of Prof. Sykes' own formula about the Anglican attitude to episcopacy, as founded on 'history,' and a claim that it has the support of Lightfoot, Stubbs, and the Lambeth Committee just mentioned.

The 'norm' being thus established, Prof. S. proceeds to the second part of his last chapter, which deals with possibilities of and actual proposals and schemes for unification with non-episcopal bodies. The direct relation of the 'norm' to this subject is not explicitly stated, but it seems to be implied that episcopacy, thus divested of any trace of doctrinal significance, will prove less of a barrier to non-episcopal bodies. The chapter concludes with two further repetitions of the norm, reinforced by quotations from Dean Swift and Dr. Johnson. The implication appears to be that in any future negotiations for unification with non-episcopal bodies, it must be recognized and admitted by Anglicans that it is anti-historical and therefore indefensible to adopt any other view of episcopacy than that it has lasted a long time—since the apostolic age to the present. This, then, seems to be the manner in which the norm is to be 'applied . . . to contemporary problems of reunion abroad and at home.'

Some of the matters dealt with in Prof. S.'s Eighth Chapter demand our attention.

As we have already seen, according to Prof. S., Tract I [1833] 'testified to the emergence of a new emphasis upon, if not a novel doctrine of, episcopacy in the Church of England' (p. 209). 'The new note struck was that episcopal ordination "marks us, *exclusively*, for God's ambassadors"' (Tract IV, qd. S., p. 210). 'It was fundamental to the Tractarian position that the validity of the

[1] The declaration [made in 1897] by the Archbishops in reply to the bull *Apostolicae curae* of 1896 is described by Prof. S. in a single phrase: 'a formal reply from the Archbishops of Canterbury and York rebutting the grounds of its argument and setting forth the Anglican doctrine of priesthood and sacrifice' (p. 229); but he does not indicate whether he thinks there can be an Anglican 'doctrine' of the priesthood without a 'doctrine' about episcopacy.

sacraments should depend upon ordination by a Bishop' (p. 210). Prof. S. maintains that these 'exclusive' claims were an advance upon those of the earlier divines, who, while staunchly defending episcopacy, 'had explicitly allowed the orders and sacraments of the foreign Protestants, who lacked Bishops' (p. 211). He does not, however, remind us, or himself, that the situation of these foreign churches might well have changed since those earlier days, and he gives no indication of whether or not those churches were still under the same 'necessity' as formerly. (I have dealt at greater length with this subject above, pp. 24, 40f.)

The attitude of the Tractarians to the 'amiable proposal' for the Jerusalem bishopric in 1841 is contrasted by Prof. S. with 'the cordial welcome given by Archbishop Sharp and other high-church bishops and clergy in the reign of Anne to the project then ventilated for the introduction of episcopacy into the churches of the Prussian territories' (p. 213). This, says Prof. S., 'was eloquent of . . . the gulf dividing [the Tractarians] from their seventeenth-century [*sic*] predecessors' (ibid.). This comment might be correct if the situation in 1841 had been substantially the same as it had been in the first decade of the 18th century; but it was not, as is abundantly clear from the citations given by Prof. S., who writes, 'Most probably Gladstone was right in seeing in the cordial support accorded to it [*sc.* the proposal] by Archbishop Howley and Bishop Blomfield "an opinion on the part of the ruling authorities of the English Church that some effort should be made to counteract the supposed excesses of the [Tractarian] party . . . by presenting to the public mind a telling idea of catholicity under some other form"' (Lathbury, *Correspondence on Church and Religion of W. E. Gladstone,* I, 229; qd. S., pp. 212–13). If this was a correct diagnosis, as Prof. S. seems to believe, the motive of the 19th-century proposal was quite different from that of the earlier one; and further, the later proposal, instead of being directed towards the healing of a breach, might well have resulted, as Pusey feared, in producing 'a heretical succession' (qd. S., p. 213). Although, therefore, Prof. S. has himself called attention to the difference of motive between the supporters of the two proposals, he does not conclude that this may explain and even justify the difference between the reactions to the proposals. He draws quite another conclusion, and one which is not warranted by the evidence which he quotes: his conclusion is that 'a gulf [divided the Tractarians] from their seventeenth-century predecessors.' It is naïve to record the difference between the two situations and then to represent the difference between the two reactions as though it were something unexpected, and to suggest that the Tractarians' reaction is somehow culpable. This is a striking example of Professor Sykes' method: he quite frankly quotes evidence which tells against his predetermined conclusion, but does not allow that evidence in any way to modify his conclusion.

Frederick Denison Maurice, however, says Prof. S., sounded 'the authentic accents of traditional high-churchmanship' (p. 215). He supported the Jerusalem bishopric proposal because he wanted 'our Protestant brethren [to] unite with us on Catholic principles and for Catholic objects'; further, he said, 'We cannot then recognize a Church without bishops. . . . It is not charity to tell you that you have not lost the sense of being members of a Catholic body, for your wisest men know that you have' (*Three Letters to the Revd. W. Palmer* [January, 1842, probably written 1841]; qd. S., p. 214). Maurice's accents were certainly explicit enough in favour of episcopacy as essential to the Church, and it is not clear how Prof. S. supposes him to be more 'authentic' (i.e. less 'exclusive') than the Tractarians with whom he appears to be contrasting him.

Archbishop Sumner, who [in 1851] in reply to an unknown and *mala-fide* correspondent had said that he hardly imagined 'there were two bishops on the bench or one clergyman in fifty . . . who would deny the validity of the orders of these clergy [*sc.* of the foreign Protestant churches], solely on account of their wanting the imposition of hands,' soon found that he was mistaken: 220 clergy of the diocese of Exeter earnestly recorded 'their conviction . . . that they only can be deemed validly ordained who have received the laying on of hands by those to whom the apostolic succession has descended' (*A letter to the Archdeacon of Totnes, by Henry Phillpotts, Lord Bishop of Exeter;* qd. S., pp. 215–16).

A controversy followed the admission of nonconformists, including a Unitarian minister, to communion at Westminster Abbey before the beginning of the revision of the Authorized Version in June, 1870. Prof. S. seems to regard this event as an instance of the 'historic attitude' of the Church of England to occasional conformity; but it is not clear whether he himself commends the inclusion of Unitarians. It may be remarked here that neither in this passage, nor in the previous passage (pp. 138ff.), where he refers to this subject, does Prof. S. attempt to supply any reasons on which occasional conformity could be justified, though his description of it as a 'healing custom' suggests that he favours it. It is not immediately self-evident in what way such a practice can be 'healing' if the occasional conformers still 'apprehend themselves bound in conscience ordinarily to separate from' the Church of England, as they did in the days of Edmund Calamy (see above, p. 45, *A Historical Account,* I, 473; qd. S., p. 138), and if, as for instance in 1870 and again in 1913, such a practice causes much 'furious controversy.'

The burking, or begging, of such an important question by Prof. S. again helps to give an atmosphere of superficiality and even of prejudice to his work; for here we see an instance of his attempting to commend a practice without investigating its significance and implications. In such comments we detect the influence of a type of liberalism, which is always ready to make free with that which is valued by others, without understanding what it is or why they value it.

13. The Twentieth Century

IN 1913 the 'reverberations' of Bishop Weston's 'characteristic protest' against the 'united' communion conducted by Bishop Peel of Mombasa in a Scottish church 'were speedily muffled by the outbreak of war,' but Archbishop Davidson produced 'a typically judicious and balanced statement of the traditional Anglican position: ". . . the threefold ministry comes down to us from apostolic times . . . we believe it to be the right method of church government . . . we believe further that the proper method of ordination is by duly consecrated bishops. . . . But to maintain that witness with all steadfastness is not the same thing as to place of necessity *extra ecclesiam* every system and every body of men who follow a different use, however careful, strict, and orderly their plan. The words and acts of many leading high-churchmen in Caroline days . . . throw a grave *onus probandi* upon those who contend for the rigid and uncompromising maintenance of the absolutely exclusive rule"' (S., p. 223). 'The lapse of a further generation,' says Prof. S. (p. 224), 'since the end of that [the 1914–18] war has not seen [the] successful realization' of the discharge of this *onus* by the 'rigorists.' Prof. S. does not point out that, while Archbishop Davidson, in stating that the right method of ordination is by bishops and that non-episcopalians are not *extra ecclesiam,* is following in the tradition of Bramhall and others (as we saw, pp. 26ff.), these beliefs do not automatically or of necessity entail the admission of non-episcopalians and even non-Christians to the *sacra* of the Church. It is this confusion which is at the root of much discussion during these last decades: it is the assumption that, because God's grace is given to those who follow some 'careful, strict, and orderly plan' other than the episcopal order, therefore somehow this plan acquires an independent and significant standing, that somehow it becomes habilitated in its own right, and that account must henceforward be taken of it on equal terms with episcopacy. The same notion is expressed from the other side in the instructions given to its Committee by the General Assembly of the Church of Scotland for communication to the Church of England in 1934: 'Any agreement with regard to the Orders and Sacraments of the conferring churches can only be based on the recognition of equal validity of the Orders and Sacraments of both churches, and of the equal standing of the accepted communicants and ordained ministers in each' (Bell, *Documents,* 3rd series, p. 122; qd. S., p. 226). So long as this attitude prevails, it is difficult to see how any advance can be made towards unification. Nevertheless, it may be that some of the difficulty is due to the ambiguity of 'validity,' and that a clearer realization of what is implied may help to find a way through this impasse.

After an account of conferences with the Church of Scotland, of the Malines conversations, and of the negotiations entered into with foreign episcopal churches and the results accruing therefrom, Prof. S. proceeds to review what has occurred during the present century on what he calls the 'home front.' Here the results have been far more meagre. At various conferences with non-episcopal bodies between 1908 and 1920, an 'impasse' had 'divided the participants on the vexed question of episcopacy' (p. 234). Prof. S. remarks that his survey of the approaches to reunion made during the 20th century shows that 'episcopacy constitutes still the chief barrier to agreement' (p. 237), and the response of the Lambeth Conference of 1948 to the South India scheme was 'equivocal' (ibid.); it has 'raised the query whether from the Anglican side episcopacy has not assumed the elusive characteristic of the ghost of Hamlet's father "*Hic et ubique:* then we'll shift our ground." The differences between Lambeth in 1930 and in 1948 have evoked the suspicion that in fact a particular interpretation of the historic episcopate (and not the adoption of that institution alone) is being asked of non-episcopal churches as a condition of full union or intercommunion; and further, that this interpretation is not the traditional Anglican doctrine [*sic*] of episcopacy but the exclusive theory of Tractarian *provenance* and championship' (pp. 237–8). 'Between the Lambeth Conferences of 1920 and 1948 there may seem, therefore, to be a great gulf fixed in respect of the requirements relating to the historic episcopate, which challenges explanation' (p. 242). Prof. S. then proceeds to his attack upon the alleged 'prevalence of a theological temper antipathetic to history,' which we have noticed already. Historically, 'the Church of England has never set forth any theological or doctrinal theory of episcopacy, but in its Articles, the Preface to the Ordinal, and the writings of its representative divines has contented itself with a historical statement of its intention to continue the threefold ministry, on the ground of its tradition in the Church since the apostolic age. As Lightfoot observed in the conclusion of his essay (on the Christian Ministry, in *Philippians* [1868], p. 267):

> If the preceding investigation be substantially correct, the threefold ministry can be traced to Apostolic direction; and short of an express statement we can possess no better assurance of a Divine appointment or at least a Divine sanction. If the facts do not allow us to unchurch other Christian communities differently organized, they may at least justify our jealous adhesion to a polity derived from this source' (S., p. 244).

It will be seen at once that Lightfoot's remarks, which Prof. S. quotes as though they supported his contention that the only Anglican ground for episcopacy is its historic continuance since the apostolic age, in fact do nothing of the sort: they contain a much more significant assertion, and they are in striking agreement with the views expressed by the Anglican divines of the Elizabethan age (and, for instance, by Bramhall), which Prof. S. has quoted earlier in his book (see p. 36, above). It is the ascription by these writers of a divine appointment or a divine sanction to episcopacy which Prof. S. consistently seeks to omit, and in the passage just quoted he has done this with even greater boldness than before. We find a precisely similar procedure on the page next following (p. 245), where he writes: 'The traditional Anglican position in regard to episcopacy therefore commends it on the strength of its long historical continuance since the apostolic age, as being of the *bene* or *plene esse* of the church; and consequently a condition of union of other churches with itself. The Lambeth Quadrilateral required acceptance of this historic episcopate, and Stubbs in 1890 offered a gloss on the phrase to the effect that[1]

> the historic episcopate, not merely as a method of church government—in which sense it could scarcely be called historic—but as a distinct, substantive, and historical transmission of the commission of the apostles, in and by which our Lord formed His disciples through all generations into a distinctly organized body or church—the historic episcopate is of the very essence of the Church of England.'

It does not need the eye of a trained historian to see that an assertion that episcopacy is 'of the very essence' of the Church is a different thing from an assertion that it is only of the *bene esse* or the *plene esse* of the Church, or to see that the 'historic episcopate' on which Stubbs is offering a gloss is an entirely different thing from what Prof. S. has been describing in his previous sentence.

[1] The following quotation is from W. Stubbs (1890), *Visitation Charges*, ed. Holmes, 1904, p. 130.

Nor is Prof. S. correct in equating his own 'historic episcopate' with that of which the Lambeth Quadrilateral required acceptance, as is clearly shown by the quotations which he himself gives from the pronouncements of the two Lambeth Conferences of 1888 and 1930. These statements are as follows:

(1) 'The Historic Episcopate, locally adapted in the methods of its administration to the varying needs of the nations and peoples called of God into the unity of His Church' (from the 'Lambeth Quadrilateral' Conference of 1888; qd. S., p. 219). This was one of the four Articles which the Conference thought supplied 'a basis on which approach may be by God's blessing made towards Home Reunion.'

(2) 'When we speak of the Historic Episcopate, we mean the episcopate as it emerged in the clear light of history from the time when definite evidence begins to be available. . . . If the episcopate, as we find it established universally by the end of the second century, was the result of a like process of adaptation and growth in the organism of the Church [*sc.* like that of the canon of Scripture and of the creeds], that would be no evidence that it lacked divine authority, but rather that the life of the Spirit within the Church had found it to be the most appropriate organ for the functions which it discharged. . . . As an institution, it was, and is, characterized by succession in two forms: the succession in office, and the succession in consecration. And it had generally recognized functions: the general superintendence of the Church and more especially of the clergy; the maintenance of unity in the one Eucharist; the ordination of men to the ministry; the safeguarding of the Faith; and the administration of discipline' (From the report of the Committee on the Unity of the Church, appointed by the Lambeth Conference of 1930; Bell, *Documents,* 3rd series, pp. 7–10; qd. S., p. 239).

It will readily be seen that neither the statement by Stubbs nor the statement of the 1930 Lambeth Committee gives the slightest support to Prof. Sykes' contention that the only ground for the commendation and acceptance of episcopacy is that of long historic continuance and that no particular interpretation of the historic episcopate is proper in the Church of England. In particular we should notice that Prof. S. ignores the very clear references to divine operation in relation to episcopacy which occur both in the statement by Stubbs and in that of the Conference Committee. In doing so he is following the practice which he has adopted with the statements by Anglican writers and authorities of preceding centuries. There is no justification whatever for his claim that the statement by Stubbs and the statement by the 1930 Conference

Committee are affirmations of his own view of what is meant by the 'historic episcopate.'

As we saw earlier (p. 12 above), it is in connection with the statement of the 1930 Lambeth Committee that Prof. S. appeals, for the only time in his book, to pre-Reformation history in order to criticize post-Reformation Anglican expressions of opinion. His reason for doing so appears to be that in asserting the establishment of the conception of episcopal succession (i.e. succession in consecration as well as succession in office) by the end of the second century, the Committee came dangerously near accepting the 'Tractarian' doctrine of episcopacy, which is distasteful to Prof. S. Although this particular appeal behind post-Reformation Anglican history is, naturally, one which is valuable to Prof. S., as tending to discredit a view with which he personally disagrees, we must not suppose that he intends us to attach too much weight to it, for, as we saw, his professed purpose is not to evaluate the historical or theological correctness of the views expressed by post-Reformation Anglican authorities, but merely to use them as independent and self-subsisting data from which an 'Anglican norm' may be constructed. For this purpose their correctness, whether from an historical or theological point of view, is irrelevant, and elsewhere in his book is consistently treated as irrelevant by Prof. Sykes.

14. Schemes for Unification

AFTER claiming corroboration of his theory by the quotations from Lightfoot, Stubbs, and the Lambeth 1930 Committee,[1] Professor Sykes proceeds, in the second part of his last chapter, to discuss various hypothetical and actual schemes for unification.

(1) First, with Presbyterian and other non-episcopal bodies. With regard to jurisdiction, 'no insuperable difficulties may be anticipated in a fusion of episcopal and presbyterian church orders' (p. 246), provided that the episcopate is not only 'historic' but also constitutional. 'The acceptance of episcopacy by the presbyterian and other non-episcopal churches would involve indeed the abandonment of the principle of parity of ministers' (!) (p. 247); but, after all, the Church of Scotland has Moderators; so, too, have 'such champions of independency as the Congregational Union'; this 'implies a tacit acceptance of imparity. And the taking of episcopacy into their systems would be the allowance of a moderate imparity.' One incidental convenience resulting from a union of the Church of England and the Church of Scotland might be a considerable multiplication of the number of dioceses in England, which 'would pro-

[1] For a further reference to the last-named passage, see pp. 68f., below.

vide a solution for the present anomaly of suffragan bishops.' Other difficulties and details are discussed by Prof. S., but he does not, indeed he cannot, claim that in modern cases any factor of 'necessity' is involved; though it may be that we are intended to regard as equivalent to 'necessity' the 'extraordinary situation' in South India to meet which the Lambeth Conference of 1930 is said to have approved consecration *per saltum* as an 'emergency measure.' Prof. S. records that after joint conferences with Free-churchmen following the Lambeth Appeal of 1920 the Anglican bishops produced a statement in which they made an explicit distinction between 'real ministries of Christ's word and sacraments' and ministries which 'may be in varying degrees irregular or defective.' We may add that in making such a distinction they were of course following the tradition of the 16th and 17th centuries.

But the practical difficulty arises with regard to the *potestas ordinis,* for the tiresome Act of Uniformity of 1662 forbids any one not episcopally ordained to consecrate the Eucharist in Anglican churches. Hence full intercommunion is not attainable along these lines, and this difficulty has 'led to the search for other means of unification' (p. 252).

(2) One alternative is conditional reordination of non-episcopal ministers; but, apart from the fact that this is 'essentially unilateral,' there is an 'essential obstacle,' which was succinctly stated by Stubbs in 1890 and has ruled conditional reordination 'out of practical consideration as a means of effecting the desired union between an episcopal and a presbyterian church' (p. 253). Stubbs remarked that it seemed unreasonable to ask presbyterian ministers to accept conditional reordination: 'the very essence of presbyterianism is presbytery; and the essence of historical presbyterianism is the negation of historical episcopacy.' In saying this he pointed out that he 'threw no doubt on their constitutional consistency or on their spiritual work' (qd. S., p. 253). We may add that herein Stubbs was following the traditional Anglican standpoint as expounded by Taylor, Thorndike, and others.

(3) Thirdly, proposals which provide 'by mutual commissioning for a complete integration of the ministries of episcopal and presbyteral churches from the inauguration of an union.' Under this head are mentioned the Proposed Scheme of Church Union in Ceylon of 1947, and the Plan of Church Union in North India and Pakistan of 1951, revised 1954. Both these schemes provide for an episcopate that shall be at once 'constitutional' and 'historic.' Their formulae, however, imply that consecration in itself gives a bishop a narrower *episkope* than he requires in the united church: his authority needs to be supplemented:

> Forasmuch as you have been consecrated to the office and order of a Bishop *in the Church of God* . . . we acknowledge you on behalf of the uniting churches, and commission you for *the wider exercise of your ministry* in the Church of God (Ceylon Scheme, 1947; qd. S., p. 254; my italics).

Similar wording occurs in the formula for Presbyters, and also in the corresponding formulae in the North India Plan. In the latter case, indeed, the *existing* bishops and presbyters have to be given 'the additional authority that they lack in separation' (qd. S., pp. 255–6); and it seems clear that the authority conferred on the ministers by consecration or ordination is not to be regarded as complete, or sufficiently 'wide' (whatever that may mean), unless they are supplied with some further authority which purports to be conferred by the 'uniting churches.'

It is not clear whether Prof. S. himself approves these proposals; but I think the reader is intended to infer that he does. In this case it would appear that Prof. Sykes must be reckoned among those who hold a view similar to the thesis of the authors of *The Historic Episcopate,* which was previously propounded by Dr. O. C. Quick (*The Christian Sacraments,* p. 145), namely, that 'in a divided Church the validity of orders becomes inevitably a matter of degree,' and that the authority of the ministers is derived from the particular 'Church' in which they function. The question then arises of who constitute the 'Church,' for it is essential to know who precisely is conferring the authority. Any one, therefore, who holds the thesis is involved in the obligation to supply a definition of the 'Church' in this connection (e.g. does the 'Church' consist simply of all baptized persons?); and this, as I have endeavoured to show elsewhere,[1] presents a problem to which it is impossible to find a satisfactory solution. Prof. S., however, shows no awareness that any such problem exists.

(4) The fourth approach is that suggested by the present Archbishop of Canterbury at Cambridge in 1946, and examined by a joint conference of Anglicans and Free-churchmen. The objective here was 'not the organic union of the several participating churches, but the taking of episcopacy into their own ecclesiastical polity by the non-episcopal churches and the creation thereby of a series of overlapping episcopal churches and ministries' (S., pp. 257–8). This scheme, however, ran into the same difficulty that confronted the South India scheme, viz., 'the failure to secure a complete interchangeability of ministries and full intercommunion' (S., p. 258).

The book concludes, as I have already said, with a final twofold

[1] In *This Church of Christ* (Mowbrays, 1955). Cf. Part II, below.

repetition of Prof. Sykes' 'norm,' and a claim that it has been voiced by 'a great and continuing cloud of witnesses,' of whom Dean Swift and Dr. Johnson are cited as having given perhaps its 'best statement.'

Perhaps the most seriously disturbing feature in Prof. Sykes' treatment of schemes for unification is his assumption (though it is not peculiar to him) that unification itself is the primary end to be achieved, that episcopacy is a 'barrier' to its achievement, and that some formula of compromise is the proper way to break down that barrier. It is, no doubt, towards the attainment of this end that he propounds his theory that 'no particular interpretation' of the historic episcopate must be asked for, but merely the adoption of that institution alone (p. 238). To this requirement he would surely expect us to add that the adoption of his own 'interpretation,' if such it should rightly be called, should be required, viz. that episcopacy is to be accepted on the sole ground of its historical continuance since the apostolic age.

The same preoccupation with unification determines Prof. Sykes' vagueness about what is meant by the Church, although he does not state explicitly in this connection, as he does in the case of episcopacy, that no theory or doctrine of it is admissible. In fact, however, he neither states nor suggests any theory or doctrine of the Church; as we have seen, he appears to be unaware that any theory or doctrine of it is needed. Thus the basis of the proposal which he offers for the unification of the various Christian bodies includes no clear notion of what the Church is, and explicitly excludes any clear notion of what episcopacy is: indeed, vagueness on these two important matters is of the very *esse* of his proposal. His proposal cannot therefore claim the serious attention of any except those who are satisfied with a vague and incoherent notion of what the Church is and of what episcopacy is and of their mutual relationship. To all others his proposal will appear as what it really is: an attempt, by one who has misunderstood the true tradition of historical post-Reformation Anglicanism as shown by the authors whose works he cites, to impose an arbitrary and inadequately documented dogma upon the Church of England. Our foregoing examination of Prof. Sykes' book has provided ample justification for this judgment upon it, and the following chapter will exhibit this even more clearly.

15. The Cloud of Witnesses

PROFESSOR Sykes' contention that the Anglican view of episcopacy is that its sole justification is its 'long historical continuance since the apostolic age' may at first sight appear plausible, for, not unexpectedly, many Anglican writers claim such continuance. It is, indeed, obviously a true claim. But it is not the whole of their claim; and it is the remainder of that claim which Prof. S. systematically eliminates. We find the claim, not merely that episcopacy has had historical continuance since the apostolic age, but that episcopacy is itself an apostolic institution, made repeatedly by the writers whom Prof. S. quotes, and many of them maintain further that episcopacy is a divine institution. In order that there may be no mistake about this, I add below some of the phrases used and statements made about episcopacy in quotations given by Prof. S. (the page references are to his book):

p. 23 'ordained of God' (Hooker).

ibid. 'the first institution of bishops was from heaven, was even of God, the Holy Ghost was the author of it' (Hooker).

p. 24 'an institution apostolical and divine' (Whitgift).

p. 62 '*optimam et divinam*'; '*ab ipso Domino instituta*'; '*Apostolos nihil constituisse in Ecclesia quod a Domino non acceperint certum est*'; '*Episcopi sunt divina institutione et apostolica traditione instituti*' (Saravia).

p. 63 'the office of bishops . . . hath authority and confirmation from God' (Sutcliffe).

ibid. 'that order which Jesus Christ prescribed, the Apostles diligently observed and maintained' (Sutcliffe).

p. 64 'we must observe and mark what manner of external government the Lord hath best liked and allowed in His Church, even from the beginning' (Bilson).

p. 66 'the divine right of episcopacy' (Hall).

ibid. 'that government, whose foundation is laid by Christ, and whose fabric is raised by the Apostles, is of Divine Institution' (Hall).

ibid. 'episcopacy is an eminent order of sacred function, appointed by the Holy Ghost in the evangelical church' (Hall).

p. 67 'the calling of bishops, as far as it is *divino jure,* cannot be taken away' (Laud).

ibid. 'there is a distinction between Bishop and Priest, and that *divino jure*' (Andrewes).

p. 68 'Christ did by the direction of the Holy Ghost and ministry of His Apostles, ordain in the New Testament, that there should be . . . bishops of a superior degree. . .' (Overall).

ibid. 'although we had not proved the immediate divine institution of episcopal power over presbyters and the whole flock, yet episcopacy is not less than an apostolical ordinance . . . which the Church hath entertained upon the confidence of that which we call the faith of a Christian, whose Master is truth itself' (Taylor).

p. 69 'That the government of the churches of Christ by bishops is of Divine Right in that first and stricter sense is an opinion at least of great probability, and such as may more easily and upon better grounds be defended than confuted'; though it would be sufficient to maintain 'that it is (as it certainly is) of Divine Right in the latter and larger signification, that is to say, of Apostolical institution . . . according to the will of our Lord Jesus Christ, and by virtue of the commission they [*sc.* the Apostles] had received from Him' (Sanderson).

p. 71 'what function or government is of apostolical institution, that is to be acknowledged a divine ordinance in respect of the first institution, as having God the author thereof; the episcopal function . . . is of apostolical institution, therefore the episcopal function is a divine ordinance' (Downham).

p. 74 'of divine right' (Andrewes).

ibid. 'of divine authority' (Andrewes).

p. 75 'a divine institution' (Hall).

p. 106 'those . . . ministers which God Himself hath made of ordinary and absolute necessity' (Taylor).

p. 147 '*disciplinam auctoritate plusquam humana fundatam*' (Oxford *Responsio,* 1706).

p. 165 'episcopacy was instituted by the followers of Christ [i.e. the Apostles] and the possessors of the Holy Spirit' (Heber).

p. 170 'this divine commission can only be had from such particular persons as God has appointed to give it' (Law).

p. 173 'the divine ordinances cannot be administered to effect but by God's own appointment; at first by His immediate appointment, and afterwards by succession etc.' (G. Horne).

p. 174 'if not expressly communicated to [the apostles] by Christ in person, must be considered established under the direction of the Holy Spirit' (Daubeny).

p. 239 'If the episcopate, as we find it established universally by the end of the second century, was the result of a like process of adaptation and growth . . . that would be no evidence that it lacked divine authority, but rather that the life of the Spirit within the Church had found it to be the most appropriate organ . . .' (Committee of Lambeth Conference 1930).

p. 244 'the threefold ministry can be traced to Apostolic direction; and short of an express statement we can possess no better assurance of a Divine appointment or at least a Divine sanction'. (Lightfoot).

p. 245 'a distinct, substantive, and historical transmission of the commission of the apostles, in and by which our Lord formed His disciples through all generations into a distinctly organized body or church' (Stubbs, definition of the 'historic episcopate').

And, as we have seen, it is no derogation from such views if any of those who held them also 'admitted' that in cases of necessity God operated through other means than those which he had expressly appointed.

We must now consider what authorities Prof. S. adduces for his 'typical Anglican norm' about episcopacy, viz. that the Anglican Church commends it solely on the ground of its long historical continuance since the apostolic age (see S., pp. 245, 261, etc.); for, as we saw, we shall naturally expect to find this norm clearly enunciated by at least a substantial minority of the authorities quoted by him if we are to admit his claim that it is indeed the typical Anglican norm.

Here, however, we at once run into a difficulty, for it is no easy matter to find such enunciations; and some statements which at first sight look promising turn out not to qualify, some because they add further grounds in support of episcopacy, a few because they express indifference to the nature of the ministry altogether, and some for other reasons.

We have already noticed that Prof. S., in first formulating his norm (S., pp. 23–8), claims that it is based on the statements of Whitgift and Hooker, whom he represents as deducing the divine authority of episcopacy from its 'historic tradition from the apostolic age' to their own times. We also saw that this was a misinterpretation of those authors' words; though even if it had been a correct interpretation, their ascription of divine authority to episcopacy would still have had to be taken into account, and they would still have said more than Prof. S. has included in his definitive versions of the norm.

What Prof. S. must be able to show, in order to prove his thesis, is an unequivocal statement by a substantial number of Anglican authorities that the sole ground upon which the Anglican Church commends, or accepts, episcopacy is its long historical continuance since the apostolic age, to the exclusion of any other consideration, and in particular to the exclusion of any assertion of the divine authority of episcopacy.

On this score the following authors must, clearly, be ruled out:

Benjamin Hoadly, who, according to Prof. S., denied that Christ delegated authority to any officers in the Church: 'little discernment was needed to perceive that Hoadly had subverted . . . all visible polity and order in the Church' (S., pp. 167–8).

Thomas Haweis, who (S., p. 172) hoped 'there are but few . . . who suppose that a Lutheran Superintendent or a Huguenot Pastor are not as truly ordained by Christ and His Church as the Archbishop of Canterbury or the Moderator of the General Assembly,' and wrote 'Respecting the administration of this Church, I am not convinced that the Lord of life and glory left any precise regulations.'

William Paley, who held that 'the apostolic directions which are preserved in the writings of the New Testament seem to exclude no ecclesiastical constitution which the experience and more instructed judgement of future ages might find it expedient to adopt' (S., p. 169).

It seems doubtful whether such sentiments can reasonably be construed as asserting that episcopacy is justified solely by its long historical continuance since the apostolic age.

I give below those quotations which might perhaps at first reading be held to qualify as explicit denials that there is any other ground for episcopacy in the Anglican Church than its long historical continuance since the apostolic age; with some comments.

(1) Bancroft (Sermon preached at Paul's Cross, 1588) said that 'the Church of God, ever since the Apostles' times, hath distributed the ecclesiastical ministry principally into these three parts, Bishops, Priests, and Deacons' (qd. S., pp. 25–6).

The qualification of this statement, however, is doubtful, since Bancroft is here arguing against the Presbyterians; and Prof. S. himself says that Bancroft defended episcopacy 'as being of apostolical provenance' (S., p. 26). Further, Prof. S. asserts that on this matter Bancroft 'ranged himself firmly behind Jewel' (p. 25), of whom he writes a few pages later (p. 28), 'For Jewel [and others] episcopacy had proved itself of divine authority by its continuance from the apostolic age until their own times.' It appears, therefore, according to Prof. S., that Bancroft did not intend to exclude the attribution of divine authority to episcopacy.

(2) Wake (S., p. 97), in replying to Pierre François Le Courayer, who had discovered that Grindal nearly 150 years earlier had licensed John Morrison, a presbyterially ordained minister, to officiate throughout the province of Canterbury, 'admitted the fact, but denied the inference' (S., ibid.), and in the course of his letter said that he was convinced that episcopacy 'has been the government established in the Christian Church from the very time of the Apostles'; and pointed out that no such licence as that which Grindal had given to Morrison would be permissible at the time of writing. On another occasion, writing to the same correspondent, says Prof. S. (p. 82), Wake 'appealed to the writings of Bridges,

Sutcliffe, Saravia and Bilson, to establish the fact that the 16th century Anglicans "learnedly pleaded the cause of episcopacy and defended the distinction of bishops and presbyters and their succession from the Apostles' times and hands."' The reference to the Apostles' *hands* seems to imply that Wake subscribed to the belief that episcopal ordination was an apostolic institution. Again, writing to the same correspondent (S., p. 122), Wake said, 'I know no government older than Calvin's time, but what was episcopal, in the Church of Christ.' It is not evident from these statements that Wake supposed the sole ground for episcopacy was its long historical continuance since the apostolic age.

(3) Perhaps a less ambiguous statement may be discerned in the letter of Dr. William Nicholls to Professor Pictet of Geneva, dated 1708, in which he says that no man when ordained in the Church of England is 'obliged by the obligation of an oath to accept episcopacy as ordained by divine right. . . . There is nothing in that Liturgy nor in its rubrics which asserts in so many words (*verbis directis*) the divine right of Episcopacy.[1] In the Preface to the formularies of Ordination it is merely stated that "It is evident unto all men diligently reading the Holy Scripture and ancient Authors, that from the Apostles' time there have been these Orders of Ministers in Christ's Church : Bishops, Priests, and Deacons." Even this clause,' continued Nicholls, 'which only in slight degree (*minime*) affirms the divine right of episcopacy, is not read in church' (S., p. 127). Nicholls also remarked, 'What private individuals think on this matter is of little importance.'

(4) 'In a Form of Service for the reception of converts into the Church of England, drawn up by Convocation in 1714, if the candidate had been a teacher in a nonconformist congregation, he was only required to "allow and approve of the orders of bishops, priests, and deacons as what have been in the Church from the time of the Apostles"' (S., p. 128).[2]

(5) The incident of the 'united communion' in East Africa in 1913 provoked a comment from Archbishop Davidson, in which he said that 'the threefold ministry comes down to us from apostolic times, and we reverently maintain it as an essential element in our own historic system. . . . We believe it to be the right method of Church government. . . . We believe further that the proper method

[1] In this statement he was, however, mistaken; see below, p. 71.

[2] This and the quotation from Nicholls are two of the three quotations given by Prof. S. to illustrate 'the theory [*sic*] of episcopacy to which Anglicans were committed by their insistence on episcopal ordination for ministry in their Church.' The third is a statement made by Wake to Prof. Turrettini of Geneva that the 36th Article 'only asserts the validity of our Book of Ordination, but does not affirm the necessity of the three Orders which we retain in our Church' (S., p. 127).

of ordination is by duly consecrated bishops' (qd. S., p. 223). The Archbishop's purpose, however, in the passage from which these remarks are taken, was to deprecate the notion that all non-episcopalians are *extra ecclesiam*; and he does not in fact here undertake to give the ground of the beliefs in the 'right' and 'proper' methods.

(6) At the Lambeth Conference of 1930, according to Prof. S., it was agreed, in reference to the proposed scheme for union in South India, that acceptance *de facto* of the historic episcopate should not involve 'any one particular interpretation of it' (S., p. 235).

(7) Prof. S. states that certain conclusions set forth by some Swedish churchmen were 'regarded as satisfactory by the Anglican bishops' at the Lambeth Conference of 1920. The Swedish writers said that

> 'no particular organisation of the church and of its ministry is instituted *jure divino*. . . . Our [*sc.* the Swedish] church cannot recognize any essential difference *jure divino* of aim and authority between the two or three [*sic*] Orders into which the ministry of grace may have been divided *jure humano* for the benefit and convenience of the church';

from which, says Prof. S., it followed that the episcopal succession in the church of Sweden was regarded [apparently by the Swedes] 'with the reverence due to a venerable legacy from the past' and as 'a blessing from the God of history accorded to us' (qd. S., p. 242; I deal with this passage more fully below, pp. 73–4).

(8) A statement by the Lambeth Conference Committee on the Unity of the Church, 1930: 'What we uphold is the episcopate, maintained in successive generations by continuity of succession and consecration, as it has been throughout the history of the Church from the earliest times, and discharging those functions which from the earliest times it has discharged' (qd. S., p. 246).

This last passage is of particular interest. It seems, perhaps, to come nearer to an explicit statement of Prof. Sykes' own position than some of the other passages which he quotes. Furthermore, it is placed by him at a significant point: it comes at the conclusion of the first part of his last chapter, just before he asks the question, 'What, then, may be required of the Anglican Church and of non-episcopal churches desiring to effect a union by mutual acceptance of "the historic episcopate"?' with which he opens his discussion of methods and schemes of union between the Church of England and non-episcopal bodies. It also follows close upon a double repetition of Prof. Sykes' own doctrine about the Anglican view of episcopacy:

> The Church of England has never set forth any theological or doctrinal theory of episcopacy, but . . . has contented itself with

> a historical statement of its intention to continue the threefold ministry, on the ground of its tradition in the Church since the apostolic age (p. 244);

and

> The traditional Anglican position . . . therefore commends [episcopacy] on the strength of its long historical continuance since the apostolic age (p. 245).

This double repetition is accompanied by a categorical identification of that view with the 'historic episcopate' of the Lambeth Quadrilateral, and by a claim that the view he holds is supported by Lightfoot and Stubbs. We have already seen that these claims have no justification. Nor does the present quotation, no. (8) above, from the 1930 Lambeth Conference Committee, bear the meaning which, placed where it is in Prof. Sykes' argument, it appears, or may appear, at first sight to bear: it may, as it stands, appear to assert just this 'long historical continuance since the apostolic age' and nothing more. Prof. Sykes has separated it from its context, and has used it to form as it were the coping-stone of the edifice which he has been constructing throughout his book. But, as the reference given in his footnote shows, it is part of the same statement as that from which the quotation on p. 239 was taken, and in that passage the Committee used the following words:

> . . . that would be no evidence that [the episcopate] lacked divine authority, but rather that the life of the Spirit within the Church had found it to be the most appropriate organ for the functions which it discharged. (I have quoted this passage more fully at p. 58, above.)

The passage, then, which Prof. S. has cited as the final and conclusive statement from a Lambeth Conference Committee in favour of his own theory, turns out to be nothing of the sort; and its use in this position, divorced from its context, has no more justification than the claim that his theory has the support of Lightfoot and Stubbs.

These eight passages, so far as it seems possible to ascertain from the quotations given in Prof. Sykes' book, appear to represent the maximum volume of the 'great and continuing cloud of witnesses to the Anglican *via media* in respect of episcopacy' (p. 260), the *via media* which 'affirms the acceptance' of episcopacy by the Church of England 'on the ground of historic continuance since the apostolic age' (p. 261). It would not be an unreasonable comment to say that the cloud does not appear to be very great or continuing, that even where it is discernible it is hardly more than a wisp, that at no point does it obscure the brilliance of the series of affirmations by 'representative divines' that episcopacy is of divine authority, and that the longer we look at the cloud the less substantial it becomes. It is difficult, in view of this almost complete lack of evidence, to concede that Prof. Sykes has proved his thesis. His formula, which is repeated over and over again in the course of the book, that the only ground on which the Anglican Church accepts and commends episcopacy, is 'its historic continuance since the apostolic age,' is a travesty of the traditional post-Reformation Anglican view as shown in the quotations which he himself provides. It cannot be substantiated by the historical evidence offered, with which it is, as we have seen, patently at variance; and we have therefore the melancholy duty of pronouncing that in Prof. Sykes' case it is not 'historical incertitude' but historical certitude which he has attempted to dispel 'by dogmatic presupposition and assertion' (cf. S., p. 243). Here indeed, in *Old Priest and New Presbyter,* Manning has come into his own, and the dogma has conquered history. In this case, however, the dogma has been devised not in order to support papal claims but in order to facilitate schemes of unification: no doubt a more worthy objective, but not one which should need the help of such means to attain it. And indeed, if such means are needed to attain the objective, we are compelled to ask ourselves whether the task is being set about in the right way, and even whether the kind of unification envisaged is a satisfactory one. Serious misgivings are produced on this score by the whole tenor of Prof. Sykes' book, which one searches in vain for any indication that the writer is aware of the nature of the Church or of the character of episcopacy, or indeed of the historic function of the Church in mediating the benefits of Christ's passion to the human race. Schemes and negotiations for union are described as though they were to be conducted between joint-stock companies contemplating amalgamation; and in order to bring about such amalgamation episcopacy is to be emptied of any significant content and adopted formally as a basis of compromise, as something about which no assertion may be made except that it has continued a long time. Not only has Prof. Sykes failed to formulate accurately the sense of what his authorities have actually said, but he has also failed to understand what it is that they are talking about. The methods to be employed for unification are entirely secular, and no reference is made to the true causes of present disunion or to the specifically Christian methods for overcoming sin and its consequences. I should have said, no reference is made *in the text of the book,* for there are two such references in quotations. The first occurs in a passage cited from Bishop Hall, but for another purpose (viz. to show that Hall did not 'blush to follow' Andrewes), in which Hall writes, 'Where then that [*sc.* necessity] may be justly pleaded, we shall not be wanting both in our pity and in our prayers' (Hall, *Works* X, 245 [*Episcopacy by Divine Right asserted*, 1640]; qd. S., p. 75). Necessity is not the only misfortune to which Christian communities are subject that calls for our pity and our prayers; and Hall has pointed us to a better way than 'the temerarious procedure' (categorically condemned but persistently pursued by Prof. S.) 'of going beyond the historical evidence and imposing dogmatic premisses upon insecure foundations' (S., p. 245). That better way was also discerned and commended by the first Lambeth Conference in 1867, which 'solemnly recorded its conviction

> that unity will be most effectually promoted by maintaining the Faith in its purity and integrity, as taught in the Holy Scriptures, held by the Primitive Church, summed up in the Creeds, and affirmed by the undisputed General Councils, and by drawing each of us closer to our common Lord, by giving ourselves to much prayer and intercession, by the cultivation of a spirit of charity, and a love of the Lord's appearing' (qd. S., p. 219).

Here indeed is the authentic road that leads towards the attainment of true unity.

Before leaving the subject of evidence, it should be noticed that an interesting piece of evidence exists in the Anglican Ordinal, which has been overlooked by Prof. S., as it was overlooked in 1708 by Dr. William Nicholls. On pp. 11–12 Prof. S. quotes the Preface to the Ordinal, and in a note (p. 12) he deprecates the emphasis which some commentators have placed upon the rubrics in the Ordinal relating to the ordination of deacons and priests, requiring that there shall on these occasions be a sermon 'declaring the duty and office of such as come to be admitted Deacons [or Priests]; how necessary that Order is in the Church of Christ.' As there is no such rubric in the Form for the Consecration of Bishops, Prof. S. has the satisfaction of pointing out that 'it may be a matter of delicacy to account for the lack of such provision at the consecration of a bishop.' It is, however, pertinent to observe that the proper Collect at the Ordering of Deacons[1] opens with the following address and petition:

> Almighty God, who by thy divine providence hast appointed divers Orders of Ministers in thy Church, and didst inspire thine Apostles to choose into the Order of Deacons the first Martyr Saint Stephen, with others: Mercifully behold these thy servants now called to the like office and administration, etc.

[1] From 1550 until 1662 this Collect occurred at a different point in the rite, both in the Ordering of Deacons and the Ordering of Priests.

The Collect at the Ordering of Priests opens as follows:

> Almighty God, giver of all good things, who by thy Holy Spirit hast appointed divers Orders of Ministers in thy Church: Mercifully behold these thy servants now called to the Office of Priesthood, etc.

A similar prayer, though it occurs at a different point in the rite, is found in the Form for the Consecration of Bishops. The address is identical with that of the Collect in the Ordering of Priests, and it then continues:

> Mercifully behold this thy servant now called to the work and ministry of a Bishop, etc.

If it is proper in this connection to follow the maxim *lex orandi, lex credendi,* we have here excellent authority for the oft-repeated belief of the Anglican divines quoted by Prof. S., who ascribe the institution of the divers Orders of the Ministry to divine operation through the Holy Spirit.

Whence, then, is Professor Sykes' 'typical Anglican norm' derived? Its real source is disclosed by the heading (and contents) of his final chapter: '*Via media:* A moderate imparity.' So far as the Anglican writers quoted by Prof. S. are concerned, there is no need to arrive at a 'highest common factor' between parity and imparity of ministers; for the number and quality of Anglican writers who advocate a parity of ministers is, as we have seen, negligible (see p. 18, above). Prof. S.'s norm represents a 'highest common factor,' not between 'various and contrasting schools of churchmanship' (p. 175) among Anglicans, but between Anglicans and certain non-Anglicans; and it is Prof. S.'s ultimate purpose of producing such a norm which determines his formulations of it throughout the book. The norm is also, presumably, intended to attract a certain type of Anglican, and also and especially non-Anglicans. For the Anglican who does not examine the formula too closely, the word 'apostolic' contains a suggestion (though *not* an assertion) that episcopacy is an apostolic institution; the word 'historic' seems to hint at the 'historic episcopate,' but without the implications of divine authority included in the elucidations of that phrase by Stubbs (qd. p. 245, see p. 45, above) and by the Committee of the 1930 Lambeth Conference (qd. S., p. 239; see p. 58 above); and the whole phrase 'historic continuance since the apostolic age' might perhaps pass muster in a dim light for a paraphrase of 'the apostolic succession.' For the non-episcopalian the formula is even more attractive, since it claims merely that episcopacy has gone on during the time between the apostolic age and the present, without any awkward mention of a 'theological or doctrinal theory' about it (p. 244); it asserts that the Anglican

Church puts it forward as a domestic requirement, and desires its restoration to those churches which have 'lost' it (without any suggestion that some of them may have rejected it); and finally it asserts that in spite of its 'loss' the non-episcopal ministries and sacraments are still 'valid.' There seems to be nothing, or very little, here which could possibly be objectionable to any non-episcopalian; and we cannot but wonder why, if this has always been the Anglican norm, episcopacy has continued to be a 'barrier' to reunion for so long. We cannot, however, withhold admiration of the brilliance of the formula, for it bears a sufficient superficial resemblance to statements made by Anglican divines which have been quoted in the book to suggest that it is based upon them, while at the same time it gives a completely different turn to their meaning. That is why it is important to examine carefully, as we have tried to do, the statements by Anglican writers upon which this norm is ostensibly based, or its continual repetition during the course of Prof. Sykes' book will mesmerize its readers, as it has mesmerized its author, into believing that the norm correctly represents the views of those writers.

We have already[1] noticed one important point on which Prof. S. differs from the authors of *The Historic Episcopate*—in rejecting the notion that there must be a theological interpretation of episcopacy. He differs from them in another significant respect. Whereas they make no secret of their admiration of episcopacy, which they extol in the most laudatory terms, Prof. S. is on the whole noticeably reticent. Episcopacy is, for him, just something which has had a long historical continuance. It is just one of those things which, as a matter of historic fact, have happened—an accident of history. Can we ascertain whether he thinks it has been a happy accident or an unhappy one? If we may judge from the few hints which Prof. S. gives us, it seems more likely that he thinks it has been an unhappy one. Although when in less melancholy mood he can endorse the view expressed by some Swedish churchmen in a Report presented to the Lambeth Conference of 1920, in which they describe episcopal succession as 'a venerable legacy from the past' and as 'a blessing from the God of history accorded to us' (qd. S., p. 242), his more usual opinion appears to be that the value of episcopacy has been exaggerated, and that it has proved more of a nuisance than a blessing. As we have seen, he twice refers to it as a 'ghost' (pp. 159 and 237); and once he describes it as constituting 'still the chief barrier to agreement' upon reunion (p. 237). Nevertheless, it is perhaps fairer to allow pride of place to his more optimistic mood; and if episcopal succession is indeed 'a blessing from

[1] p. 25, note 2, above.

the God of history,' what has become of Prof. Sykes' careful elimination from his norm of the statements of Anglican writers asserting the divine origin and authority of episcopacy? Must we, then, after all, reckon Prof. S.'s endorsement of the Swedish view as a comment made in an unguarded moment? It is difficult to be certain; but if we look at the context we shall see that the phrase which Prof. S. commends is presented as following from the view that 'no particular organization of the Church and of its ministry is instituted *jure divino,* not even the order and discipline and state of things recorded in the New Testament. . . . Our [i.e. the Swedish] church cannot recognize any essential difference *jure divino* of aim and authority between the two or three Orders into which the ministry of grace may have been divided *jure humano* for the benefit of the Church' (qd. S., p. 242). It would seem, therefore, that in commending the phrase mentioned, Prof. S. is regarding it as a figure of speech, and not as attributing any *jus divinum* to episcopacy.

In conclusion, some of the results of our examination of Prof. Sykes' book may be stated as follows:

Professor Sykes has attached unwarranted importance to temporal duration in making the following assumptions:

(1) that the prevalence of a theory or an attitude for 400 years is in itself a sufficient guarantee of its correctness;

(2) that the long continuance of an institution is in itself a sufficient ground for commending its acceptance.

These two assumptions are closely interconnected in Prof. Sykes' book, since the particular instance of (1) with which he is concerned is the alleged post-Reformation Anglican 'attitude' towards episcopacy, viz. that the sole ground for commending episcopacy is of the type mentioned at (2) above, viz. its 'long historical continuance since the apostolic age.'

It has been shown that the evidence quoted by Prof. Sykes

(1) does not support his thesis that the post-Reformation Anglican attitude towards episcopacy is that the sole ground for commending its acceptance is its 'long historical continuance since the apostolic age';

(2) exhibits a much more positive doctrine about episcopacy in post-Reformation Anglican writers.

It has been argued that, even if Prof. Sykes' thesis had been satisfactorily established,

(1) such a ground for commending episcopacy would not of itself be sufficient;

(2) the opinion that it was sufficient would not be binding upon all Anglicans for all future time.

PART II

VALIDITY

IN view of the ambiguity of the term 'validity' as often used, and the confusions and misunderstandings which frequently result from it, I have endeavoured in this second Part to examine the subject rather more fully than was possible in the first Part of the book.

The principle which I mentioned above in Chapters 8 and 9, namely, that in all sacraments it is God who is the 'validator,' and that sacraments are occasions for the operation of God upon human souls, is fundamental for a right understanding of sacraments and their 'validity.' It is for this reason that such terms as 'validity' and 'efficacy,' as they are commonly used, are apt to be dangerous and misleading, because they tend to encourage those who use them to overlook the essentially personal nature of the sacraments. There are a number of errors into which such an attitude may lead; a few of them are discussed below, and some suggestions made towards clarification.

(1)

THE basic weakness in many theories, both ancient and current, about the validity of sacraments is that they adopt a meaning of validity which produces a rigid demarcation between what is valid and what is invalid. This error is due to a failure to take into account what we have just mentioned, viz. the essentially personal nature of all sacraments, and, consequently, the manner in which God works upon human souls. If this is overlooked, it becomes easy to regard the question of the validity of sacraments as one which can be examined and determined by means of a quasi-legal method of examination, and this leads at once to the drawing of rigid distinctions such as that which I have already mentioned.

In the earlier periods of the Church's history, some held the view that Orders were null and void if conferred by heretics or schismatics—i.e. no *potestas* was conferred. This view, however, was opposed by S. Augustine (5th century), and he was later followed by S. Thomas Aquinas, who held that the recipients of such sacraments received the *potestas* but not the right to exercise their orders, nor the grace of them (*nullam executionem aut gratiam*). This states the contrast between sacramental validity and canonical validity; and the latter can be supplied without further difficulty when the schism or heresy which precluded it has been removed: orders which (to use more modern terms) are *valid* though *irregular* can be *regularized*. No doubt the reason which gave rise to this contrast was the importance attached to the maintenance of unity and orthodoxy in the Church; and although it may therefore have been a matter rather of policy than of theology, the Church, as we shall see, is an important factor when we consider the question of the efficacy of Orders. The theory just stated, however, purports to determine in precise terms what is the effect of heresy and schism upon the operation of a sacrament; and this is particularly noticeable when we see that it explicitly denies that *grace* is conveyed through orders conferred by heretics or schismatics. This is a denial which is on quite a different level from the denial that such orders convey the right to exercise the power conferred. During the first ten centuries, apart from S. Augustine, there was a strong tendency to recognize no distinction between what would now be called 'invalidity' and 'irregularity,' and some Orders were treated as 'invalid' which later would have been treated merely as 'irregular.' This tendency, again, was no doubt mainly due to the importance attached to the suppression of heresy, schism, simony, and other similar evils; nevertheless, this view, even more than the other (which ultimately prevailed), presumes to make an absolutely clear-cut distinction between 'valid' and 'invalid.'

In these earlier centuries, of course, no problem arises of non-episcopal ministries; all the orders conferred purported to be the recognized Catholic episcopal orders. In Reformation and post-Reformation times, however, we are confronted with the emergence and perpetuation of non-episcopal ministries. These ministries may be classed under two main headings:

(a) non-episcopal ministries deliberately set up as such, involving a deliberate break with the traditional ministry, perhaps owing to conscientious objection to the corruption observable in those who then exercised it;

(b) non-episcopal ministries adopted unwillingly owing to pressure brought to bear by external authorities which would not permit the perpetuation of the traditional ministry.

We should perhaps add to these a third class,

(c) non-episcopal ministries originally adopted under (a) or (b) and retained and perpetuated after the conscientious reason or the *force majeure* has ceased to operate.

In the case of (a), the theory of the ministry involved is a novel one, and was apparently originated by Luther, who in 1523 advised the Bohemian Utraquists to forgo the requirement of episcopal ordination, and to 'choose pastors for themselves.' It is the theory that the Christian congregation can of itself evolve and empower a ministry, as opposed to the view that the ministry is derived from the commission given by the Lord through the Apostles and the Episcopate—the doctrine commonly known as that of the Apostolic succession. It is essential to keep in mind the fundamental difference between these two theories of the ministry, for some modern schemes for unification confuse them or fail clearly to distinguish them. They are however mutually incompatible, because they involve quite different conceptions of the nature of the Church. This point does not concern us at the moment, but the question of the 'validity' of congregationally-authorized ministries does. On the Thomistic view, all such ministries are unmistakably 'invalid'; and it is here that we begin to feel that the term 'invalid' (which came into common use later than S. Thomas) is misleading, since it appears to suggest, and in practice can hardly fail (and is often meant) to suggest, that such ministries and the sacraments administered by them cannot be 'efficacious,' and this implication appears even more unsatisfactory in the case of non-episcopal ministries which were adopted involuntarily owing to external pressure. It would therefore not be unreasonable to regard with favour the view of W. Bright, quoted by Dr. B. J. Kidd (*Theology*, January, 1937): 'To say, however, that Orders, or Sacraments in general, are invalid or null, does not mean that they are inefficacious; and besides the distinction between validity and regularity, we must make a further distinction between the validity and the efficacy of Christian ordinances. . . . We hold that they [*sc.* who receive communion at a Eucharist which is not administered by a priest] do not indeed receive the sacred gift contained in, and conveyed by, a valid Eucharist; but that if they come with right dispositions to the Lord's Supper, it becomes to them an occasion of communion with God and Christ, which, being on their part earnest and sincere, cannot possibly fail to be accompanied with blessing. . . . Eucharists so-called administered by those who are not priests, and ordinations so-called administered by those who are not bishops, are *invalid* for lack of due authority in the ministrant, *but* they may be *efficacious* in the sense of being the means or occasions of spiritual fellowship with God which is certain to win a blessing.' This view, as Dr. Kidd remarks, is in some measure similar to that expressed by S. Thomas, who wrote (*Summa,* III^a^ pars, Suppl. Q, xxxviij, Art. 2) *et ideo alii dicunt quod vera sacramenta conferunt, sed cum iis gratiam non dant, non propter inefficaciam sacramentorum, sed propter peccata recipientium ab eis sacramenta contra prohibitionem Ecclesiae. Et haec est tertia opinio; quae est vera.*

The principle involved in these views is clear, but it will be argued below that the terminology is still misleading. S. Thomas' statement purports to distinguish between reality (cf. *vera*) and efficacy (cf. *non propter inefficaciam*) on the one hand, and the conferring of grace (cf. *gratiam non dant*) on the other. It is, to say the least, confusing to hold that a sacrament may be valid (*verum*) and efficacious, yet fail to convey grace; or that although a sacrament may be invalid it may yet be efficacious, and while unable to convey grace may yet be able to convey blessing. This difficulty arises from the attempt to specify over-precisely what happens in a sacrament, and it seems doubtful whether any intelligible or practical meaning can be attached to the distinction between conveying grace and conveying a blessing. A clue to the solution of the difficulty is given by the mention of the Church in the passage quoted from S. Thomas; but here again the phraseology is too rigid, for it seems doubtful whether the 'prohibition of the Church' can be competent to control the conveying and the withholding of grace. Nevertheless, there is a valuable truth contained in the statement, for, as we shall see, the ability of the Sacraments to convey grace is in a very real sense dependent upon the character of the community in which they are celebrated and received, though the fixing of the two mutually exclusive alternatives 'grace within the Church, no grace outside the Church' is too rigid. The true solution to these problems is to be sought not in an attempt to determine precise lines of demarcation with regard to what is valid and what invalid, what is efficacious and what is not efficacious, what conveys grace and what does not, but in the light of the essentially *personal* character of the sacraments, and indeed of the Church itself and of the whole scheme of salvation, and particularly through a consideration of what is the divine will with regard to the nature of the Christian ministry. Our aim, therefore, will be not to determine the precise point at which validity or efficacy ceases, or at which grace ceases to be conveyed, but to understand what is the will of God with regard to the Christian ministry. It will not help us to repeat with the authors of the *Memorandum on the status of the existing Free Church Ministry* (1923):

> Ministries which imply a sincere intention to preach Christ's Word and administer the Sacraments as Christ has ordained, and to which authority so to do has been solemnly given by the Church concerned, are real ministries of Christ's Word and Sacraments in the Universal Church. Yet ministries, even when so regarded, may be in varying degrees irregular or defective.

This statement is the result of a desire on the part of its authors to avoid the use of the terms 'valid' and 'invalid,' but it includes some terms whose meaning is obscure (e.g. 'real,' 'Universal Church'), and it appears to admit the view that 'the Church concerned' is competent to give authority to a (non-episcopal) ministry. So far as the statement is intended to safeguard the principle that such ministries do not administer nothing, it can be regarded sympathetically; but its description of them as 'irregular or defective' is not sufficiently explicit or informative; and it must, as we shall see, be emended so as to assert that such ministries 'are not those which have been divinely appointed.'[1] This, indeed, is the fundamental question which must be faced in all discussions about unification; it is not 'Have these ministries been ("in varying degrees") blessed by God?' but 'What is the ministry which God has appointed?'

The modern Roman argument against the Anglican Church does not entirely coincide with any of the views which have been already mentioned, although it has some affinities with them. Briefly, the argument is that it is possible for certain motions, let us say the motions of the consecration of a bishop, to be gone through, and yet, owing to some alleged defect of form, of matter, or of intention, or because the Pope has decided that nothing shall happen,

[1] Cf. above, pp. 29ff.

nothing really happens: the 'sacrament' does not 'mediate any efficacy' and is incapable of doing so; it is not 'efficacious' and no order is conferred. Comparable instances would be going through the motions of working the handle of a pump, and failing to raise any water because there was no water in the well; or the *bona fide* sale of a theatre ticket which turned out to be a forgery. It is unnecessary at this point to examine the reasons which lead Roman Catholics to adopt such a position—they are sufficiently well known. The presuppositions and implications, however, of that position now demand our attention.

What is the conception of 'validity' which it implies? It will be seen that, like many other theories about validity, it attaches paramount importance to what may be called the technical framework of the sacrament, i.e. to the part played in it by human beings in fulfilling certain prescribed requirements. This attitude tends to produce a narrow and legalistic conception of the operation of sacraments, and leads to thinking of each sacrament as an isolated event, and to the attempt to define precisely what happens in it, with the result of excluding from consideration its fundamentally personal aspect as an operation of God upon or for human souls. Such an operation is not something which is instantaneously completed, and its effect cannot be confined within the duration of the performance of the sacramental rite. The sacrament must be considered in its setting in the whole life of the individual concerned, and in the whole life of the Church in which the individual is placed.

Our consideration, then, so far suggests that it is not satisfactory to apply the term 'validity' exclusively or even primarily to the technical framework (the matter, form, and intention) of a sacrament, which represents the immediate requirements for its performance on the human side. This will be brought out more fully if we consider the matter in greater detail.

Unlike the effects brought about by physical actions, the effects brought about by sacramental actions are not susceptible of any obvious or immediate independent verification. There is no independent means of ascertaining, by an inspection or examination of the persons or objects concerned, whether a man has or has not been ordained priest, or whether a piece of bread has or has not been eucharistically consecrated, any more than there exists an independent means of ascertaining whether two people have shaken hands or made each other a promise, or whether a certain article has been given as a present by one friend to another.

What criteria, then, can be adopted for deciding whether or not a sacramental act is, or has been, 'valid'? Are we to defer a decision until there has been opportunity to examine appropriate evidence and thereby to decide whether the results which might be expected to follow from a 'valid' sacrament have in fact been produced? This can hardly be regarded as a satisfactory method for several reasons, and in particular because it might be difficult to prove that any observed results were in fact due solely and directly to the sacrament. In any case, such a method would not enable us to tell beforehand whether any particular sacramental act was going to be performed in such a way that it would be 'valid,' and consequently able to produce the appropriate results.

In default of a satisfactory objective method of verification after the event, it has become customary to adopt criteria which can be applied before and during the event; hence the well-known criteria relating to form, matter, and intention. Are these satisfactory criteria for the 'validity' of a sacrament?

We may begin by observing that if there are to be sacraments at all, there must clearly be certain requirements with regard to the actions performed, the things used, the words spoken, and the intention with which the whole is done; but it seems reasonable to suppose that whatever these requirements are, they will have been made as simple as possible in order that the divine operation may have as free a passage and as universal an availability as possible. The purpose of sacraments must be to enable divine power and grace to be the more readily mediated to men; they are intended to be channels of supply and not opportunities for obstruction and deception. It would therefore seem to be misguided to look upon the sacramental form, matter, and intention as hurdles set up by God (and if they are not set up by Him, what justification have they?), which have to be successfully cleared before He is willing to allow any efficacy to be mediated, hurdles which have been carefully designed to trip up non-specialists, who may not, e.g., know the precise theological terms in which they should mentally frame their intention, although they have a sincere intention to act in conformity with the command of Christ. If we consider the actual form and matter of the various sacraments, it appears to be the case that they are indeed of patent simplicity. And even with regard to the third factor, the intention,

> people who are not theologians [so a well-known Roman writer informs us[1]], never seem to understand how little *intention* is wanted for a sacrament (the point applies equally to minister and subject). The 'implicit intention of doing what Christ instituted' means so vague and small a thing that one can hardly help having it—unless one deliberately excludes it.

[1] Adrian Fortescue, *The Greek Fathers,* p. 94, n. 2.

But even if there should be some failure on this score,

> relying on the promises of her Founder [so another Roman writer assures us[1]], the Church knows that the Holy Spirit will provide that no serious breach will occur in her succession of Orders and valid sacraments.

This sentiment appears to be unexceptionable, and there is no obvious reason why such a provision should apply exclusively to the Roman Church. Can we detect here a belated recognition that Roman arguments against Anglican orders have been following a line which can never be convincing? Those arguments have continually shifted their ground as they have been successively refuted; and this in itself indicates the difficulty of establishing a case against 'validity' on the score of form, matter, and intention. Although they continue to be repeated by controversialists, the Roman arguments are now discredited, and it is difficult, as Fr. Clark finds, to produce an argument against Anglican Orders which might not apply also against Roman Orders. Indeed, the statement which I have quoted above indicates that a line of argument independent of form, matter, and intention has to be resorted to if Roman Orders are to be successfully guaranteed; and similarly another independent line of argument is required to 'invalidate' Anglican Orders: as stated by Fr. Clark,

> the [Roman] Church has an effective power to restrict sacramental validity (op. cit., p. 10).

I make no further comment on this statement at present. We need only note here that this principle by-passes the requirements of form, matter, and intention.

I have raised these points, not to suggest that form, matter, and intention are unimportant, but to show that they are, as no doubt they were intended by God to be, the simplest and most easily satisfied of the requirements involved in the use of sacraments. It is difficult to believe that they were intended to be made the basis of attack by one Christian body against another as has been done for the past few centuries by the Roman Church.

In the preceding paragraphs I have been thinking chiefly of Christian bodies which uphold the doctrine that sacraments are effectual means of grace. There are of course some Christian bodies which do not uphold this doctrine, but there seems no adequate reason why the provision enunciated by Fr. Clark should not in principle apply to all Christian bodies, for they all have some serious intention of obeying the Lord's commands when they perform their sacramental rites and, as Bright observed, this obedience

[1] Francis Clark, S.J., *Anglican Orders and Defect of Intention* (1956), p. 61.

in itself cannot go unrewarded. It is difficult to believe that the Holy Spirit, while ensuring that nothing goes 'seriously' wrong with Roman sacraments, deliberately ignores the sacraments of those Christians who do not subscribe to the papal claims, or that He has no concern with the Breaking of Bread on a Sunday morning at a meeting of Plymouth Brethren. However imperfect the intention may be on the part of those who perform or participate in the sacraments, it is the same God in whose name and in obedience to whose commands they are performed; and to suppose that all sacraments not papally recognized are null and void, or to suppose that God does nothing in response to the human performance of them, is to attribute to Him a callousness of which any normal human being might be ashamed. If it be suggested that some distinction must be drawn between 'covenanted' and 'uncovenanted' grace, we must ask in what precisely the difference between these consists. It cannot be seriously maintained that God has two different reservoirs of grace, one for Roman Catholics and another for Christians who are not Roman Catholics, and that the latter is somehow of inferior quality to the former. We shall see later how this problem should be restated, and how it can be solved.

The error in the view which locates 'validity' in the human fulfilment of certain technical requirements (form, matter, intention) is that it overlooks the true purpose of sacraments, concentrates upon a narrowly limited aspect of what is required on the human side, leaves out of account the divine aspect, and ultimately leaves out of account the nature of God Himself. It assumes that if a prescribed recipe is followed, if certain ingredients are used, if certain actions are performed, then the result is automatic—*sacramentum conficitur,* and we have a 'valid' sacrament. Such a view might be appropriate if in sacraments we were concerned with physical ingredients whose nature is such that when, and only when, they are mixed in certain proportions and treated in certain ways, they immediately produce a certain result. Much controversial language about validity appears to assume that sacraments are concerned with materials of this sort. But if it is God Himself who is the source of the efficacy mediated by sacraments, and if it is His grace, and in a sense Himself, that is mediated by them, it is incredible that He should not mediate as much of His grace and power, or as much of Himself, as can possibly be mediated by them; and that whatever limitations or obstructions there are will be due not to Him, nor to human sincerity however ignorant, but to other impediments which partake more obviously of the nature of sin; and from such impediments Roman Catholics are no freer than other Christians. It seems reasonable to suppose that whenever men, in response to what they believe to be God's command, provide Him with an opportunity for the mediation of His grace, such as the performance of a sacramental rite appears intended to be, He will make the fullest possible use of that opportunity. The action of God will not necessarily wait upon the attainment of punctilious technical correctness, as Fr. Clark rightly remarks.

It is this kind of consideration which amply vindicates the line taken by the Anglican divines of the 16th and 17th centuries, who recognized the 'validity' of the sacraments of those continental churches which, though prevented from following the traditional and divinely-appointed methods, honestly and in good faith continued as best they could in those oppressive circumstances. Those divines realized that it is God only who can validate sacraments, for it is He who operates through all sacraments, and it is within no man's competence to say that God does not, or shall not, so operate. We must then reject the notion that the validity of sacraments is something which can be gauged without reference to the nature of God and His purpose in the sacraments; and also the notion that the validity of sacraments can be 'controlled' by the arbitrary pronouncements of an ecclesiastical authority, as is claimed by the Jesuit writer already quoted.[1]

The effect, if not the deliberate intention, of Roman arguments about 'validity' and 'invalidity' is to concentrate attention upon the immediate technical requirements on the human side, and thereby to suggest, or even to affirm, that only those sacraments which satisfy the conditions which may at any time be papally prescribed, or only those sacraments which are certified by papal *fiat,* are capable of mediating grace. As soon as we reduce the technical requirements to their proper proportions in the whole scheme, it becomes possible to take into account the nature of God as the 'validator' of all sacraments, and to allow requirements for 'efficacy' which are of a character other than technical to assume their proper importance; and some of these requirements are of such a nature that they cannot be supplied by any kind of authorization or *fiat,* papal or other.

It is, then, grossly misleading and dangerous to connect the notion of 'validity' with the immediate technical requirements on the human side, and it makes a balanced view of the operation of sacraments almost impossible. The validity of sacraments should be regarded as something which is dependent not upon any human

[1] F. Clark, op. cit., p. 10. According to him, the Pope, in the constitution *Apostolicae curae,* rejected the Anglican ordination rite 'as incapable of mediating sacramental efficacy' on the ground that 'the [R.C.] Church has an effective power to restrict sacramental validity.'

contribution but solely and wholly upon God's willingness to respond, i.e., it depends upon the source and giver of the gift conveyed, and not upon the means by which it is conveyed. The technical requirements are comparable with the simple action of stretching out the hand to receive the gift which God is waiting to give—an essential movement, of course, but not one which provides, *or is intended to provide,* opportunity for miscarriage. It is the appropriation and use of the gift which is the important requirement on the human side, and it is upon man's ability and willingness to appropriate the gift that the 'efficacy' of sacraments in the true sense depends. We may thus include under factors affecting the 'efficacy' of sacraments all the considerations which in earlier times or at the present day have been held to inhibit or hinder the conveyance of *potestas,* or of grace—heresy, schism, irregularity, etc., whatever it may be, as well as moral defectiveness in the individual recipient. All these things in varying degrees impede the operation of God through the sacraments, but in no case are we entitled to say that they completely impede it, and therefore we may not say 'No grace is conveyed here,' 'no efficacy is mediated here,' and so forth. Such assertions derive from the supposition that it is possible to state in precise terms what happens in any sacrament, and this in turn presupposes the use of subpersonal terminology in stating what is alleged to happen. This point will be dealt with more fully presently.

We have, then, two agents concerned in every sacrament, the divine and the human, God and man. On the one side, God is the source of *validity* in its proper sense : He is the supplier of the grace and power. On the other side, man is required to fulfil certain simple technical requirements (to say certain words, to perform certain actions, etc.), and beyond that, he has to appropriate the grace and power in order that the sacrament may be in the true sense *efficacious.* For man, the first set of requirements is easily met; the second is more difficult. To use the terms 'valid' and 'efficacious' in any other senses than these can only cause confusion and lead to a distorted conception of the sacramental system and God's purpose in it. It can also, as we know from experience, give rise to unedifying controversy. The writers of the *Memorandum* above mentioned (see p. 80) were therefore right in so far as they wished to avoid the use of the term 'valid' in its current sense; for if 'validity' is identified with technical or ritual correctness, the formulae and actions come to be regarded as having *of their own nature* the power to bring about some immediate and precisely specifiable result, as it might be a chemical reaction, directly dependent and consequent upon the nature of the ingredients concerned, and this notion leaves no room for the nature of God. And if 'efficacy' is treated as an automatic sequel to 'validity,' it is hardly possible to avoid obscuring the importance of the part which must be played by man in appropriating the gift conveyed through the sacraments.

I shall therefore take it as established that, whatever obstruction or limitation there is to the 'validity' of sacraments, it is not imposed by God as a punishment for technical defects, and that it cannot be artificially imposed by man (e.g., it is not within human competence to declare that any sacrament honestly performed is 'invalid,' that is to say that God does not convey any grace to other persons by means of it), but that the only genuine obstructions are those which automatically and because of their own intrinsic nature militate against the effectual operation of God's grace in the sense of so conditioning human souls that their receptivity of it is impaired. We must refuse to accept an arbitrary and rigid demarcation between 'valid' and 'invalid' sacraments, since we cannot admit that God is ever unwilling to supply to the full the gift which He intends to convey through the sacraments whenever they are honestly performed, and no conceivable obstacle on the human side can be an absolute bar to His operation. From what we know of the nature of God, we must assume that whenever in good faith men act in His name, however ignorant or misled they may be, He makes the fullest possible use of the opportunity which they, in the exercise of their free will, offer Him, and that He who is able to bring good out of evil is not likely to refuse to bring good out of good.

(2)

We have thus been able to locate one source of error in discussions about validity, viz. the failure to conduct the discussion in personal terminology. The same error can be described in two other ways which for convenience I will call the error of *chronological isolation* and the error of *extensional isolation.*

The contention or assumption that it is possible to draw a clear distinction between valid and invalid sacraments is closely connected with the view that it is possible to define in exact terms precisely *what happens* in any particular sacrament: this notion also derives from a failure to bear in mind the essentially personal nature of the sacraments. If, for instance, we say that the effect of baptism is to regenerate, what precisely do we mean by this? If we say that in ordination a certain 'character' is conferred, what does this mean? If we say that in the Eucharist the 'substance' of bread has been replaced by the 'substance' of our Lord's Body, what does this mean?

So long as we hold clearly in mind that through these sacraments a Person is acting upon a person, God upon human souls, we shall recognize that it is absurd to attempt to formulate in precise terms what *happens* in these sacraments; but if we lose sight of that essential aspect, we may find ourselves striving to express in less than personal terms something which transcends non-personal terminology, and in consequence we shall be asserting less than the truth, or even seriously distorting the truth.

We may now go on to state in greater detail what is implied by these subpersonal views of the sacraments, and by the allied view that it is possible to define precisely what *happens* in any sacrament. Two assumptions are implied: (a) The first assumption is that any particular sacramental act can be isolated and considered and defined as something complete in itself. In such a definition or description no time later than the duration of the performance of the rite comes into consideration; it is assumed that there is a moment when the action is complete; and it may then be asserted e.g. that this or that *has been done* to this person or to this thing. This error we may designate as the error of *chronological isolation*. It is an error which may be committed with regard to the Eucharist, a sacrament in which lifeless objects are concerned, and the question is then asked (and, of course, answered), What *has happened to* the bread and wine? It may be committed also with regard to other sacraments, where lifeless objects are not concerned (or not concerned in the same way), e.g. with regard to ordination and baptism, and the question is then asked (and answered), What *has been done to* the person in this sacrament? (b) Secondly, it is assumed that it is possible to state the effect of a sacrament in isolation from its setting in the whole life of the Christian society. In this case, no proper account is taken of the fact that the performance of a sacrament presupposes the whole corporate and continuous life of the Christian community, and that the individual sacramental act, however important and august, is not properly intelligible or significant unless it is considered as having its place in this setting. This error we may designate as the error of *extensional isolation*.

These two erroneous assumptions, although they can be distinguished and stated separately, are commonly made simultaneously, and indeed they are closely related and both are open to objection on similar grounds. They derive from the notion that a sacramental act is comparable to an isolated physical act, e.g. that of making a table, the table being complete in itself when the action has been performed; or to the act of taking a bath. In other words, they fail to take account of the essential nature of a sacramental act, which is comparable with the influence exerted by one person upon another; indeed, as already pointed out, they are a direct consequence of considering the sacraments in a subpersonal way.

We may now consider these two assumptions more fully, with examples.

(a) The error of chronological isolation.

To illustrate this we may resume the case of baptism, already mentioned. If we say that the effect of baptism is to regenerate, what precisely do we mean by this? It is unnecessary to enter upon a full theological exposition; a rough statement will suffice for our purpose. When we say that a person has been regenerated in baptism, we mean at least this: that God has accepted the baptized person, in virtue of the merits of Christ, as standing in a new and definite relationship to Himself; he is enabled to make a new start; he is born again—*in order to lead a life of a certain character*, a life in which the baptized person's will is to become progressively more closely assimilated to the will of God. If we consider the sacrament in this way, we realize at once that what happens in baptism is not an action which is complete and self-contained, but rather the beginning of a continuous divine activity, the influence of God exerted upon the life of a human soul. The action of God in baptism is above all a forward-looking action, not something self-contained and isolable, and its full significance cannot be understood or stated if it is considered as something isolated, finished, and completed at a definite moment. The same is true of every sacrament. Just as baptism is the means whereby God supplies to the human soul the grace which it requires at the beginning of its Christian career, so through every other sacrament He supplies the appropriate grace and power which the soul requires *for the time which lies before it*, to enable it to perform its Christian duty, either in general (as through Holy Communion) or for some specialized duty (as through ordination or marriage), and to make more and more perfect the assimilation of its will to His during the performance of that duty.

It is, therefore, important to think of the divine action through every sacrament as the beginning of an activity, rather than as an isolated act complete in itself; and if we consider e.g. baptism in this way we shall see that it is inadequate to say that what has happened in any particular baptism is that 'regeneration has taken place.' It is inadequate to describe this, or any sacrament, as an *opus operatum*; it is rather an *opus inchoatum*; a work, certainly, but a work which has been begun by God, and still remains to be continued and completed.

A corollary to this is that no person can claim merit in virtue of having been baptized. This follows, of course, from the fact that no person can deserve baptism, and that it is a free gift of God. But it follows also from the nature of baptism itself. What the person has received in baptism is not as it were a treasure which can be put away into a bank and cited whenever occasion arises as a permanent asset. Like a talent, it must be used; and unless it is used we cannot expect that even God Himself will count it to us for righteousness. The claim that we have Abraham to our father is not one which carries weight in the sight of God.

(It may be remarked in passing that these considerations have a direct bearing when we examine the commonly-held view that by baptism a person is made 'a member of the Church.' However edifying this statement may be, it is a metaphorical statement, and as such must be treated cautiously. It can easily lead us to suppose that something complete in itself has been accomplished at baptism, that some right has been conferred, entitling the recipient to a voice in the affairs of the Church, etc. This is only partly true. There can, of course, be no doubt that something has been done by God, and something that He will never go back on; but, as was pointed out above, baptism is the first act of God upon the soul, implying that the soul must be put in the way of receiving further acts of God upon it. The statement that baptism confers 'membership of the Church,' from its similarity to comparable phrases used of secular societies, can easily mislead us into thinking that membership of the Church is acquired on similar terms as membership of those societies, that it confers 'rights' in a similar way, and so on. But if we recall the true nature of baptism, it is difficult to see what meaning can be attached to the claim that a person is a 'member of the Church' simply on the ground that at some time in the past he was baptized, if he has never taken any further step towards living the Christian life. The notion that 'membership of the Church' is 'conferred' by baptism can be particularly dangerous in discussions about the authority of the Ministry. In recent years the theory has been revived that the authority of the ministers of the Church is derived from 'the Church'; that such authority is defective unless it has the backing of 'the whole Church'; and further that, because the Church is at present divided, no ministry can be other than defective. The weakness of this theory is disguised by the fact that there is ready to hand the plausible notion that all baptized persons are 'members of the Church' and that these constitute the 'Church' from which it is alleged the authority of the ministers is derived. The same view, viz. that it is possible to say precisely that this or that *has been accomplished* by any particular sacrament may account for some of the difficulties which are felt about the relationship of baptism to confirmation. The difficulties in all these cases can be largely ascribed to the notion that it is possible to say precisely what is effected by the sacramental act in isolation, and that whatever is effected is completed and finished at that moment.)

We may now consider the case of the Eucharist. Our Lord's description of the Eucharistic elements as His Body and Blood appears to be intended to indicate the purposes which He meant them to fulfil for the benefit of His people rather than to indicate the nature of any change which occurs in the bread and the wine at the moment of consecration; and it may be that the attempt to produce a philosophical statement of the change effected in them is to divert our attention from the true purpose and nature of the sacrament. It is not, after all, necessary to know the precise chemical composition of ordinary foods, or the precise methods by which they are made, in order to benefit by eating them: it is sufficient to know, on the strength of general human experience, or the reputation of the manufacturer, that they are wholesome for us. Similarly, it is not necessary to know how precisely one person influences another in order to benefit by association with our friends. It may indeed be impossible to produce a satisfactory statement in philosophical terminology about any sacrament, and so far as our understanding of the purpose of the sacrament of the Eucharist is concerned, and so far as our ability to benefit from reception of it is concerned, neither the doctrine of transubstantiation nor any other such doctrine takes us an inch farther. So far as the purpose for which the sacrament was instituted is concerned, all such doctrines are superfluous. Concentration upon them, or upon any one of them, merely focusses our attention on something which is entirely irrelevant, knowledge of which is no more requisite for the purpose of the sacrament than a knowledge of the pigments used by a painter is requisite for an appreciation of the picture itself. What is important is the knowledge that our Lord has chosen these things for this purpose, and that whenever we 'do this' with them according to His command, His promise will be fulfilled. That promise is not to perform some metaphysical miracle of which the relevance is by no means obvious, but to accomplish a miracle which is at once more divine and more practical—to communicate His divine power to human souls. The true meaning of 'This is my Body' is not to be elucidated in terms of scholastic or any other philosophy, but at an entirely different level.

Our question therefore must be, not 'What *happens to* the Eucharistic elements at consecration?' but 'What are the purposes which our Lord has willed to accomplish by means of them?' This is a relevant and very practical question, and the answer to it cannot be given in the terms of a statement that at a certain moment some change was brought about in the elements. It will have to be given in personal terms, and it will include mention of our Lord and of the human soul. After consecration the elements are the means whereby Christ is available to His faithful people as an object of their devotion and worship, by which He enables them to assist at the offering of His redemptive sacrifice, by which He conveys to them the merits of that sacrifice, and so forth. The act of consecration, therefore, like the act of baptizing, is not self-contained and isolated, but forward-looking, and its significance cannot be expressed in a statement which is concerned only with the time during which the act occurs, which represents that act as chronologically complete, and which confines itself to what is alleged to happen to the elements.

Indeed, if we concentrate our attention too narrowly upon what is alleged to happen to the elements, we shall encounter considerable difficulties. What precisely do we believe happens to a recipient of the Eucharist? However firmly we may believe that the 'substances' of bread and wine are replaced at consecration by the 'substances' of our Lord's Body and Blood, we are no nearer answering this question. We cannot undertake to explain what happens to these substances when the elements are received in communion, or how they act upon the soul of the recipient. The best and most satisfactory sort of answer we can give is that by receiving the Eucharistic elements the Christian soul is brought into an intimate relationship with its incarnate divine Redeemer, and receives from Him whatever grace and power it is capable of receiving. And this is an answer which can be given without having previously provided an explanation of what is supposed to have *happened to* the Eucharistic elements. It is sufficient to say that God, using the obedience and expectancy of man as shown in the act of consecration, has made those elements a means towards the diffusion of His redemptive power among men. We do not know *what happens to* the Eucharistic elements at consecration; all we know, and all we need to know, is *how God regards them* after consecration and what He purposes to do for us by means of them. We do not know precisely *what happens to* a person at baptism, but we do know how God henceforward regards that person, what is the relationship between God and him, and what God is able and intends to do henceforward with that person. In this respect we may also trace a parallel between the Holy Eucharist and Holy Order. We cannot say precisely *what happens to* a person who is consecrated bishop or ordained priest, but we know how God henceforward regards such persons, and what He intends to do for His people through those who are consecrated and ordained—just as we know what He intends to do for them through the consecrated Eucharistic species.

We see then that it is dangerously misleading to attempt to express in static and therefore subpersonal terms the gift which is conveyed through any of the sacraments. It is unnecessary to attempt to define precisely *what has been done to* the elements in the Eucharist, or *what has been done to* the recipient of them, or to the recipient of Baptism or of Holy Order. A divine activity has been begun in a particular place, for certain persons, in certain souls, and the sacraments are indeed literally *means,* means between persons, means connecting God and man.

Some of the sacramental rites which under God's providence have been provided as means for the conveyance of His grace and power for human life are intended to deal with special needs, some are more general in their purpose. Thus, among those intended for special needs, we may reckon baptism, intended for those who are beginning their life in the Christian society; confirmation for those who are reaching their coming-of-age in the Christian life; marriage for those who are to live together as man and wife. These sacraments are given at the beginning of a specialized kind of life, and not all of them are necessary to all Christians, though some are. Further, there are the sacraments of absolution and unction, for those in spiritual or bodily distress, and these are in a more direct and obvious sense remedial. Next, we have the Holy Communion, which is a gift of general application, necessary to all Christian people, and of the widest and most varied use. Lastly, the sacrament of Holy Order, comparable in one respect to marriage, in that it is designed to enable the recipient for duties of a special kind in the Christian life, duties to which not all Christians are called, and comparable in another respect with Baptism and Confirmation, in that it introduces the recipient to a more responsible stage in the Christian family life, this time, as it were, to the duty and privilege of fatherhood, enabling the bishop to beget in Christ, as S. Paul begat, new children of the Church (now only in Confirmation, but originally also in Baptism), and to beget new supporters and feeders of the Lord's families (in the ordination of priests) and their helpers (in the ordination of deacons—attendants, servants), and this reminds us that, as through the sacrament of Holy Order men are taken by Christ to act *in loco patris* in His family, so simultaneously, by the most touching and humbling of all Christian paradoxes, the Master who came on earth to be a servant takes them also to be servants on the staff of His household, to wait and attend upon the family's everyday wants and in their crises and emergencies.

General	*At the beginning of a special kind or stage of life*	*At emergencies*
Holy Communion	Baptism	Absolution
	Confirmation	Unction
	Marriage	
	Order	

Although the grace and power required at these different occasions or stages may vary, it is the same Lord who is the source, and the grace and power which He gives is nothing less than Himself, His presence, His companionship, enabling and sustaining. Each person draws what he needs, so far as he can, from the perfect sufficiency of Christ, as it were touching the hem of His garment and receiving exactly what he needs. It is inconceivable that Christ, who healed as it were unwittingly the woman who pulled at His coat, will refuse what His children need because they have pulled the wrong side of His coat or have not formulated their requests in precise and exact language. The assertion that God withholds His gift for ecclesiastically-invented reasons is the blasphemy of asserting that for bread God gives His children a stone, and for eggs scorpions. And this, essentially, is the Roman assertion and blasphemy—disguised only because instead of using personal terminology it uses abstract and non-personal terms and phrases.

(b) The error of extensional isolation.

We have now seen the importance of avoiding consideration of the sacraments in chronological isolation. The same reason as before, viz. their essentially personal nature, will show us the importance of avoiding consideration of them in *extensional isolation*. In other words, the sacraments must be thought of in their setting in the corporate life of the Christian community. They are acts of God performed upon or for individual souls, but performed within the Christian community and for souls who are living within that community.

It is not to be supposed that God deliberately withholds His grace and power from any human being, Catholic or non-Catholic, Romanist or non-Romanist, Christian or non-Christian, who earnestly desires to receive these gifts. There is much evidence to show that the gifts of God are bestowed whenever man is receptive of them. On God's side we cannot believe that there is any limit or impediment to this generosity. The impediments are found only on the human side. They may be found in the individual: they may be caused by his deficient receptiveness, in its turn caused by sin. But they may also be found in the individual's environment, in the society or community in which he lives—by the corporate defectiveness of the community. Indeed, this corporate aspect is of equal importance with the individual aspect, and the two cannot be kept separate. The nature of man, who is made in the likeness of God, presupposes certain conditions for the receiving of God's gifts, and to a Christian, one of the most obvious and most fundamental of these conditions is the life in the Christian community. No man can attain salvation privately; union with God is union with Him in a society. It is the truth expressed in the old saying, *nulla salus extra ecclesiam.* I call this a truth, for such indeed it is. God's grace is communicated to men above all in the divinely-appointed society. This society, according to Catholic belief, is the Apostolic Church, that is to say, the community whose centre and source is the Apostolic ministry, and which derives its life from God through prayer and through the word preached and the sacraments administered by those ministers in the context of the community. In no other society can God's grace be 'efficacious' as He intends it to be, and therefore in no other society can His sacraments be 'efficacious' as He intends them to be, not because God is unwilling to allow them to convey His grace and power otherwise, or because the Church has decreed that no grace or power shall be conveyed otherwise, but because it is man's nature to be saved in a society, and in a society possessing that particular nature and quality which God has bestowed upon the Apostolic Church. No other society, we believe, is adequate for this purpose, and God has provided it as the wholly adequate and appropriate society for the human race in its present condition, the society in which men may attain as nearly as possible on this earth the life for which they were intended at their creation. Properly speaking, therefore, no other society has the right to the title of 'the Church,' for this is the only society ordained of God for His redemptive purposes for mankind. Similarly, the Apostolic ministry is the only ministry which has the right to the title of stewards of the mysteries of Christ, for this is the only ministry appointed by Him. It is therefore no exaggeration on the part of the Tractarians, whose words are quoted with disapproval by Prof. Sykes (p. 210), when they claim that those who have been episcopally ordained are '*exclusively* . . . God's ambassadors' (Tract 4). They are such, not because they were ordained by a rite which was technically correct, or because episcopal ordination is an ancient tradition, but because theirs is the ministry which God has appointed to constitute the character of the society wherein His grace is to operate with the least impediment.

It is, then, in the setting of the Apostolic society that we shall see the significance of every sacrament and of the celebration of every sacrament. Nowhere else can the sacraments be 'efficacious' in the way which God intends. And this society, as we should expect, is itself a sacramental society: it is based upon the principle that God uses *means* for the bestowal of His gifts. It is a sacramental society because at its centre, as its nucleus, is the Apostolic ministry, a sacramental order of persons, persons through whom God's gifts are mediated, persons who continue the work of Christ who 'came to minister'; and this ministry is primary and fundamental, because actions presuppose persons to perform them, and since persons are prior to things and actions, the sacramental nature of the Church resides primarily and fundamentally in persons, i.e. in the Apostolic ministry.

It may also be remarked that the Church and the Ministry are mutually complementary. Although the Ministry does not derive its authority from the Church corporately, but from the Lord's commission inherent in the Apostolic office, and although the Church, under God, derives its being from the Apostolic Ministry, so that where there is no Apostolic Ministry there can be no Church, yet the existence of the Church is presupposed and implied by the existence of the Ministry, for if there is a minister there must be those to whom he ministers, and the Apostolic Orders are conferred not in private, but in the course of the Eucharist, which is a corporate act of the Christian community. Thus although the essential nucleus is the Apostolic Ministry, this Ministry itself would be meaningless without the community to which it gives existence and to which it ministers. Indeed, the structure of the Apostolic community is the pattern for all human society; for the 'greatest' are made humble because the essence of their office is to wait upon the 'least' in the Lord's family: and the 'least' are made humble, for, like Peter at the washing of the feet, unless they allow themselves to be waited upon they cannot share in the gifts which the Lord has provided.

Nevertheless, just as an individual's defects may impede the operation of God's grace, so may the defects of a society, and it is not to be supposed that even the divinely-given society will so far escape the contagion of sin that it will always and wholly fulfil God's will as intended by Him. To this extent the efficacy of the sacraments will be impeded. It is recorded of Christ that on one occasion in a certain place 'He could do no great work because of their unbelief.' This clearly refers to the attitude of the community as a whole. So, too, Christ may be here, in His Sacrament, let us say, but He may be unable to do any great work because of our unbelief. This in itself indicates the futility of allowing our attention to be monopolized by the technical 'validity' of sacraments: our formulae and our ordinations may be guaranteed 'valid' by the Vicar of Christ himself; but what value has such 'validity' if those among whom Christ comes make His presence powerless by their misbelief and sin? It is not enough that we should be sure on technical grounds that 'He is here'; we must know *who* He is that is here, and what manner of person He is, for otherwise we shall be incapable of any communion or communication with Him, and our certainty of His presence will be an empty mockery. It has, of course, been the practice of Roman controversialists in their attacks upon the Anglican Church to concentrate upon 'validity' in the technical sense and to attempt to show that on some technical point (of form, matter, or intention) Anglican Orders and therefore all other sacraments are 'invalid.' Such arguments, as they have been refuted, have successively shifted their ground, and this in itself shows their ineffectiveness; yet the attack continues, and it is sometimes difficult to resist the conclusion that the purpose of those who make them is not so much anxiety that Anglicans should not be deceived by 'invalid' sacraments as a desire to bring about the dissolution of what is regarded by them as a rival and counterfeit institution. Yet even if these Roman arguments had been sound, it would still require a separate argument to establish the 'efficacy' of the 'valid' Roman orders and sacraments, for the reasons already explained, viz. that technical 'validity' in itself is insufficient. Indeed, it is open to question whether a community, which at any rate in England appears to allow its spokesmen to denigrate the most sacred rites of another Christian community, can provide the necessary conditions in which Christian sacraments can be efficacious.

It is, therefore, entirely unnecessary for Anglicans to be disturbed by the arguments of Roman controversialists on the subject of validity. Such attempts, when deliberately made in order to unsettle simple and honest Christian people, are in themselves reprehensible; but even if they had been sound and justifiable, it would still be arguable that technically 'invalid' sacraments, if sincerely performed, are at least as likely to be truly efficacious as sacraments however technically 'valid,' performed by those who appear to think of God as the assay official of a spiritual Goldsmiths' Company, carefully scrutinizing every piece submitted to Him in the hope of finding a flaw. We may indeed be thankful that we have not so learned Christ, and that from the earliest times of the reformation in the Anglican Church a very different view has been taken of sacramental validity and efficacy. It is one of the major contributions of Prof. Sykes' book that he has produced clear evidence for this.

It is, indeed, of prime importance to remember that the beliefs of the community in which the sacraments are administered must of necessity play a substantial role so far as the efficacy of those sacraments is concerned. In the Roman Church we find that the sacramental and Apostolic office of the episcopate has been for practical purposes superseded by the autocratic office of the papacy (which is not a sacramental office at all, but merely an organizational one), and that the Pope claims to be able, without reference to fact or to reason, to add to the deposit of faith which is necessary to salvation, and arbitrarily to restrict sacramental 'validity' even in Christian communions other than his own. There is, of course, no Christian community which is free from impediments to the effectual working of the grace of God, just as there is none where that grace is entirely prevented from operating. But it is important that we should not be mesmerized into supposing that such impediments are to be found only in non-Roman communions, or that the only type of impediment is that which Roman controversialists are never tired of laying to the charge of other Christian bodies.

Summary

THE foregoing discussion has attempted to show

(1) That personal terminology only is adequate for the discussion of sacraments, and that when the discussion of them is translated into personal language it becomes impossible to state precisely *what has happened* in a sacrament. We can say that God supplies His grace and power to a person for a particular duty or for a particular need, but we cannot specify more precisely than this. We can say that henceforward Christ as redeemer is with that person, sustaining him in his particular duty, whatever it may be, as one who belongs to the society of the redeemed. This is true of those sacraments which are received when a certain course of duty is first undertaken, and these are the sacraments which are not repeated. In the case of sacraments which are received regularly, or which may be repeated, a similar thing is true, though no special duty is involved : each person's needs are different, and each person's needs are supplied. The same principle holds in the case of the consecrated material elements in the Eucharist which exist as continuing intermediaries between God and man. It is impossible to say what *has happened to* the Eucharistic elements in consecration, but it is possible to say how God henceforward regards them and what He purposes to do for men by means of them.

(2) The nature of contact between persons prevents us from formulating in precise language what God does in a sacrament; we can, however, say what is the maximum which He wishes to

give. The nature of God prevents us from asserting that owing to some defect on the human side God is unwilling to make any response at all. Whatever impediments there are to the reception by a human being of the maximum which God wishes to give, they are to be looked for e.g. in moral defectiveness in the individual or in the moral or structural defectiveness of the Christian society in which the sacraments are administered. Yet even so, all sacraments to some extent, and some sacraments primarily, are remedial.

(3) All sacramental rites, therefore, if sincerely and honestly performed, will be 'valid,' in the sense that God is always willing to respond. The term 'valid' should thus be applied to refer to this willingness of God and not to the mechanical and technical actions, words, etc., required on the human side. The latter are so simple that it is difficult not to fulfil them otherwise than deliberately, and any sincere and honest performance of them includes by implication the intention to do what God requires in this respect.

(4) Nevertheless, the provisions made by God by way of sacraments have been to some extent hindered by human sin or error, and not all Christians are willing to make use of all the divinely appointed methods. This is true in particular of the sacrament of Holy Order. Some Christians are not willing to accept the Apostolic ministry, and hence God is unable to provide them with it. Consequently, He is unable to give them the Apostolic society, which cannot exist without the Apostolic ministry. Such a society, lacking this ministry, cannot therefore be the 'Church' as properly understood, but whatever God is able to do through the ministry which such a society is willing to accept He will accomplish. A similar statement can be made, *mutatis mutandis,* about the various beliefs which are held e.g. about the Eucharist. There may be all degrees of hindrance to the effective working of God's power through the sacraments, but there is no point of which we can say : This marks the boundary between the field where God so operates and the field where He does not so operate.

(5) The term 'efficacy' should not be used to describe an alleged automatic sequel to 'validity' in the technical sense, but to describe the manner in which the true validity derived from and supplied by God in the sacraments is able to become effective in human lives. It is, in fact, unnecessary to make use of any other terms than these two : validity and efficacy. Any attempt to particularize further is misleading and implies a distortion of the situation as it really is : in other words, it fails to allow fully for the fact that in sacraments the situation is a personal one. On God's side there is validity—God's willingness to supply all that He wishes us to have through the sacrament; on the human side there are the various

impediments which either individually or corporately determine the extent to which God's desire to operate through the sacraments can be effectual.

(6) The difference between episcopal and non-episcopal ministries is not one of validity and invalidity but one of degrees of efficacy, and this is due to the fact that the divinely appointed society is the Apostolic society (the Church), of which the Apostolic ministry is the nucleus and source. Our criticism of non-episcopal ministries therefore is not that they are not 'valid' (i.e., not that God refuses to work through them), but that they are not the divinely appointed ministry, and therefore cannot constitute the Apostolic society, in which alone the conditions can be provided in which sacraments can be efficacious in the way God intends them to be.

(7) It is not possible to determine theoretically or *a priori* what is the divinely appointed ministry. This, like much of the Christian faith, must be regarded as a matter of divine revelation through the Holy Spirit. We might claim (as some have claimed) to be able to invent better methods of Church government, but that is to misunderstand the matter. Having accepted the Apostolic ministry as a divine institution we can see how this sacramental order of men constitutes the Apostolic and sacramental society. This ministry represents the Christian ministry as God intends it to be, and the conditions provided by the Apostolic society are those which God intends as best for the living of the Christian life. Anything less than the Apostolic society, or any distortion of it, will proportionately detract from its suitability to fulfil God's purpose. I make no apology for asserting that I believe the Anglican Church comes nearest to reproducing the pattern of the Apostolic society as God intends it. If I did not believe this, I should not belong to the Anglican Church. The non-episcopal communities have not the Apostolic ministry, and therefore cannot claim to be the Church in its proper sense; the Roman Church has so far lost sight of the importance of the ministry as a sacramental order that it has superimposed upon it the control of a purely organizational office (the papacy).[1] I am not so stupid, I hope, as to think the Anglican Church is perfect, any more than I think any Christian community is perfect, but it is, by the providence of God, free from these two fundamental defects, viz. the abandonment of the Apostolic ministry, and its eclipse by an autocratic non-sacramental organization, both of which defects have a direct effect upon the character of the society concerned and are prejudicial to its purpose as intended by God for the training and salvation of souls.

(8) In the light of this we can see that the notion that any one

[1] See E. L. Mascall, *Corpus Christi,* pp. 17f.

who has been baptized is once and for all a 'member of the Church' is mistaken. Baptism does not make a person once and for all a member of the Church, and the notion that it does is, in its way, as mechanical, and therefore as mistaken, as the Roman notion that only technically 'valid' sacraments can effectually mediate grace. A person is baptized because, if he is to be a Christian, there must be some occasion when God as redeemer acts upon him for the first time, and God's first such act upon him is baptism. In that sense, but only in that sense, baptism is unique among sacraments, and we must not on that account think of it in isolation. The result of our thinking of it as conferring 'membership of the Church' may result in our so thinking of it, and if we do that, we may then be thinking of it in less than personal terms. 'Membership of the Church,' if we wish to use the phrase, must not be envisaged as something static, a status once for all acquired by the act of baptism, but rather as is described in Acts 2 : 41 f., 'They then that received his [Peter's] word were baptized . . . and they continued stedfast in the Apostles' teaching and fellowship, in the breaking of bread and the prayers.' Membership of the Church is an activity, not a once-for-all-acquired status; it is life in the divine society, in communion with the Apostolic ministry, participation in the sacraments, and maintenance of the Apostolic faith.[1] The Church, then, is not a society which is constituted by a large number of baptized persons: millions of such persons might exist and yet fail to constitute the Church. The Church is constituted by God through the threefold Apostolic ministry, and those who wish to live in that society, sharing its life and learning salvation, will conform to its manners, which are also the divinely appointed means whereby God acts upon each soul. The notion that 'membership of the Church' is a status once for all acquired through baptism is responsible for much confused thinking on the subject of the unification of Christendom. It leads to the belief that all baptized persons are automatically 'members of the Church' simply in virtue of their having been baptized, and it can also provide a basis for the erroneous theory that the authority of the Ministry is derived from 'the Church,' i.e. from the whole number of baptized persons. I have endeavoured elsewhere[2] to point out some of the difficulties and absurdities inherent in this theory, though indeed they should be apparent enough.

[1] The metaphorical (and scriptural) description of baptism as a 'new birth' is a valuable one, but its limitations as a metaphor must not be overlooked. The natural birth of an infant is normally followed by a process of natural growth, which apart from accidents is regular and automatic. The 'rebirth' in baptism, though intended to initiate a process of spiritual growth, is not, unfortunately, invariably followed by such a process.

[2] In *This Church of Christ* (Mowbrays, 1955).

APPENDIX

A Table to illustrate the application of Professor Sykes' theory of 'long historical continuance' (see page 30, note 1)

In the Table below the length of historical continuance of episcopacy and of a non-episcopal ministry is given at intervals of 50 years from 1550. For the purpose of simplification, it has been assumed that episcopacy began in the year A.D. 50 and presbyterianism in A.D. 1550. The Table shows how the length of historical continuance of presbyterianism expressed as a percentage of the length of historical continuance of episcopacy is always increasing (col. 4), although the rate of increase is always diminishing (col. 5). It will be seen that whereas in 1700 the length of historical continuance of presbyterianism was only 9% of that of episcopacy, by 1950 it had risen to the alarming figure of 21%.

(1) Year A.D.	(2) Length of historical continuance (expressed in years) of Episcopacy	(3) of Presbyterianism	(4) Length of historical continuance of Presbyterianism expressed as a percentage of that of Episcopacy	(5) Increase of percentage during 50 years
1550	1500	0	0	—
1600	1550	50	3.2258	3.2258
1650	1600	100	6.25	3.0242
1700	1650	150	9.0909	2.8409
1750	1700	200	11.7647	2.6738
1800	1750	250	14.2857	2.5210
1850	1800	300	16.6667	2.3810
1900	1850	350	18.9189	2.2522
1950	1900	400	21.0526	2.1337

Similar tables could be constructed for other non-episcopal ministries. The fact is thus clearly demonstrable that, *vis-à-vis* all of these other ministries, on the score of length of historical continuance episcopacy is steadily losing ground.

INDEX

(This Index is not exhaustive; it is intended to be supplementary to the Table of Contents)